AN INTIMATE LOOK AT THE

FATHER-HEART OF GOD

# THE
# LOVE
# OF GOD

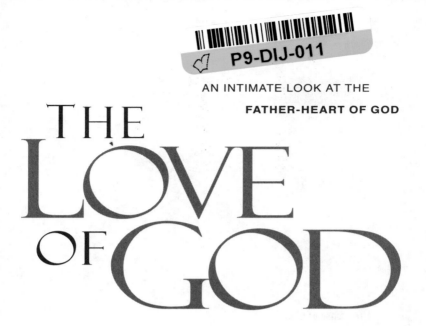

## OSWALD CHAMBERS

### Discovery House Publishers

*Books, music, and videos that feed the soul with the Word of God*

Box 3566 Grand Rapids, MI 49501

*The Love of God*

© 1938 Oswald Chambers Publications Association

This edition © 1988 Oswald Chambers Publications Association Limited.

Discovery House Publishers is affiliated with RBC Ministries, Grand Rapids, Michigan.

Discovery House books are distributed to the trade exclusively by Barbour Publishing, Inc., Uhrichsville, Ohio.

Requests for permission to quote from this book should be directed to Permissions Department, Discovery House Publishers, P.O. Box 3566, Grand Rapids, MI 49501.

Unless otherwise indicated, Scripture quotations are from The New King James Version. Copyright © 1979, 1980, 1982, Thomas Nelson Publishers, Inc.

Interior design by Limelight Graphic Design

ISBN 0-929239-04-0
89-831871

Printed in the United States of America
06 07 08 09 /DP / 16 15 14 13

# THE
# LOVE
## OF GOD

# Other Oswald Chambers books from Discovery House Publishers

# CONTENTS

## Now Is It Possible—

# Publisher's Foreword

Few Christian writers in this century seem to have tapped the spiritual realities of our biblical faith as has Oswald Chambers. Known for his bestselling devotional book *My Utmost for His Highest*, his writings have been compiled into a library of more than thirty volumes, most of which are unknown even to those who have read *My Utmost*. Because we believe the Christian community needs to rediscover Chambers, Discovery House Publishers is committed to reprinting new, updated editions of the Oswald Chambers Library. The first volume in the series is this study on *The Love of God* and related themes.

Believers need to hear again from this great devotional writer, to learn the art of biblical meditation, to reflect on the Word of God as taught by the Spirit of God, to know the mind of Christ, and to "appraise all things" from His divine perspective (1 Corinthians 2:9–16).

The author's style is brief and meditative. His work must be read slowly and contemplatively so that his words can be assimilated into one's own thought and behavior. As a theologian, Chambers is noncritical, dealing with truth as it affects us personally rather than coming to the teachings of Scripture dogmatically and critically. He assumes the absolute authority of the Word, then plumbs its depths to tap the revelation of God in a manner which generations of readers have found enriching and spiritually stretching.

We commend *The Love of God* to you, trusting that by reading it you will discover afresh the reality of faith at work, making the Father known to you, the Son real to you, the Spirit alive to you, and the Word rewarding to you.

THE PUBLISHER

# THE LOVE OF GOD

# GOD IS LOVE

He who does not love does not know God, for God is love.
(1 John 4:8)

No one but God could have revealed *that* to the world, for we all
see nothing but its contradiction in our own limited world of experience. We need little imagination to construe the life of millions of
this world's inhabitants into vehement laughter at such a declaration as "God is love." Shattered, broken lives contradict any such
statement. No wonder carnal minds consider us infatuated, mere
dreamers, talking of love when murder, war, famine, lust, pesti-
lence, and all the refinement of selfish cruelty is abroad in the earth.
But, oh, the sublimity of the Abraham-like faith that dares to place
the center of its life, confidence, action, and hope in an unseen and
apparently unknown God, saying, "God is love," in spite of all ap-
pearances to the contrary; saying, "Though He slay me, yet will I
trust Him" (Job 13:15). Such faith is counted for righteousness.

Look back over your own history as revealed to you by grace, and
you will see one central fact growing large—God is love. No matter how often your faith in such an announcement was clouded, no
matter how the pain and suffering of the moment made you speak
in a wrong mood, still this statement has borne its own evidence

along with it most persistently—God is love. In the future, when trial and difficulties await you, do not be fearful. Let not this faith slip from you—God is love; whisper it not only to your heart in its hour of darkness, but here in your corner of God's earth. Live in the belief of it; preach it by your sweetened, chastened, happy life; sing it in consecrated moments of peaceful joy; sing until the world around you "is wrought to sympathy with hopes and fears it heeded not."

The world does not bid you sing, but God does. Song is the sign of an unburdened heart; then sing your songs of love unbidden, ever rising higher and higher into a fuller concept of the greatest, grandest fact on the stage of time—God is love.

But words and emotions pass, precious as their influence may be for the time. So when the duller moments come and the mind requires something more certain and sure to consider than the memory of mere emotions and stirring sentiments, consider this revelation—the eternal fact that God is love, not, God is loving. God and love are synonymous. Love is not an attribute of God, it is God; whatever God is, love is. If your concept of love does not agree with justice, judgment, purity, and holiness, then your idea of love is wrong. It is not love you conceive of in your mind, but some vague infinite foolishness, all tears and softness and of infinite weakness.

## How Is God Love?

**In His very nature.** Some exceptionally gifted men may derive their concept of God from sources other than the Bible, but all I know of God I have learned from the Bible, and those who taught me got what they taught from the Bible. In all my dreams, imaginings, and visions I see God, but it is the God of the Bible that I see, and I feel Him to be near me. I see ever amid the mysteries of providence, grace, and creation "a Face like my face," and "a Hand like this hand," and I have learned to love God who gave me such a sure way of knowing Him and left me not to the vain imaginations of my own sin-warped intellect.

**In creation.** The love of God gives us a new method of seeing nature. His voice is on the rolling air, we see Him in the rising sun, and in the setting He is fair; in the singing of the birds, in the love of human hearts, the voice of God is in all. Had we but ears to hear the stars singing, to catch the glorious pealing anthem of praise echoing from the hills of immortality by the heavenly hosts!

**In His wisdom.** God did not create man as a puppet to please a despotic idea of His own; but out of His abundant flow of overflowing love and goodness, He created us to receive all the blessedness which He had ordained for us. He "thought" us in the rapture of His own great heart, and lo, we are! Created in the image of God were we, innocent of evil, of great God-like capacities.

**In His power.** The whole world moves but to His great inscrutable will; animate and inanimate creation, the celestial bodies moving in their orbits, the globe with all its diversified issues and accompaniments are all subservient to this end.

> Yes, God is good, in earth and sky,
> In ocean depth and swelling wood,
> Ten thousand voices ever cry,
> God made us all, and God is good.

**In His holiness.** God walked with man and talked with him, He told him His mind, and showed him the precise path in which he must walk in order to enjoy the happinesses He had ordained for him; He rejoiced in the fulness of His nature over man as His child, the offspring of His love. He left nothing unrevealed to man; He loved him. Oh, the joy and rapture of God the Father over man His son!

**In His justice.** God showed to man that compliance with His dictates would ever mean eternal bliss and joy unspeakable and life and knowledge forevermore, but that ceasing to comply would mean loss of life with God and eternal death.

That was in the world's bright morning when the morning stars sang together and all creation leaped in joy, but the wild, wild desolation of sin, disobedience, pride, and selfish sinfulness entered and drove a great gulf between God's children and Himself. But, as ever, love found a way. God came to us and for us, and we this day with chastened hearts, quivering lips, and glistening eyes, yet with love deep and strong in our hearts, say, afresh with deep adoration, God is love.

If God exhibits such glorious love in His nature, what shall we say of the glories of the dispensation of His grace? That God would have walked this earth had sin never entered is very likely, yet sin did not refrain Him from graciously walking and revealing Himself in communion with men. No, still He came. But men were so blinded by sin that they saw Him not, they knew Him not, while He hewed a way back through the hard face of sin to the heavenly shores.

## The Gift of God's Only Begotten Son

Surely Jesus Christ reveals God's love in an amazing degree. "He who did not spare His own Son" (Romans 8:32) has shown that it matters not how bad a man is; if he will but lift his eyes to the cross he shall be saved. But yet so blinded, infatuated, and imbecilic has man become by sin that he can see nothing in the life of Christ save the evidence of a beautiful, good life of a misunderstood man who suffered and died as a martyr. To meet this difficulty love Himself gave another gift.

## The Gift of the Holy Spirit

When He shines on the historic Christ, all the great and gray outlines spring into glorious relief and color and beauty, and the soul, amazed, calls out, "My Lord and my God." When the Holy Spirit has begun His gracious work in your soul and heart by making it tremulously expectant, you see a new light on the cross and the "martyr" becomes the Savior of the world.

> Surely He has borne our griefs, and carried our sorrows: yet we esteemed Him stricken, smitten by God, and afflicted. But He was wounded for *our* transgressions, He was bruised for *our* iniquities: the chastisement for *our* peace was upon Him; and by His stripes we are healed" (Isaiah 53:4–5, italics added).

Though it is too difficult, nay impossible, to trace that God is love by mere unaided human intellect, it is not impossible to the intuitions of faith. Lift up your eyes and look abroad over the whole earth, and in the administration of God's moral government you will begin to discern that God is love; that over sin, war, death, and hell He reigns supreme; that His purposes are ripening fast. We must, by holy contemplation of all we have considered, keep ourselves in the love of God; then we shall not be able to despond for long. The love of God performs a miracle of grace in graceless human hearts. Human love and lesser loves must wither into the most glorious and highest love of all—the love of God. Then we shall see not only each other's faults, we shall see the highest possibilities in each other, and shall love each other for what God will yet make of us. Nothing is too hard for God, no sin too difficult for His love to overcome, not a failure but He can make it a success.

God is love. One brief sentence; you can print it on a ring: It is the Gospel. A time is coming when the whole round world will know that God reigns and that God is love, when hell and heaven, life and death, sin and salvation, will be read and understood aright at last.

God is love. A puzzle text, to be solved slowly, as with tears and penitence, by prayer and joy, by vision and faith, and, last, by death.

# Keep Yourselves in the Love of God

Keep yourselves in the love of God, looking for the mercy of our Lord Jesus Christ unto eternal life. (Jude 21)

The love of God. We have lost it today; we have turned our back on the ocean and are looking out over barren, colorless hills for the ocean's fullness. We need converting again—turning round, and there basks the ocean, whose waves sparkle and ripple on fathomless deeps and fullnesses. We are too introspective today. We mourn and wonder; then lifted on waves of feeling, we glow and say we love God. But again our feelings ebb and flow and we mourn. Christianity is not a thing of times and seasons, but of God and faith. Drink deep and full of the love of God and you will not demand the impossible from earth's loves; then the love of wife and child, of husband and friend, will grow holier and healthier and simpler and grander.

But there are initial stages to be considered before we come to the glorious exhortation. The love of God is not revealed by intellectual discernment, it is a spiritual revelation. What ups and downs we experience because we build not on faith but on feeling, not on the finished work of Christ but on our own work and endeavor and experience.

> "But you, beloved, building yourselves up on your most holy faith" (Jude 20).

Is that what *you* are doing every day? Do you have family worship? Do you have private devotions? Do you read your Bible more and more? Can you answer "Yes" to these questions, or is a hesitant "No" given by your spirit to God? Family worship is so far off, so remote. You remember your father and mother who prayed and talked of sin and righteousness and judgment to come, but you have other things to heed; you are more enlightened; you read sceptical books, controversial books, that attack the foundations of your faith.

If these things have crept unawares into our hearts, let us get back in penitence and consider what is the foundation on which we must build our most holy faith, namely, that "God so loved the world that He gave His only begotten Son, that whoever believes in Him should not perish but have everlasting life" (John 3:16). Let us get down to the cross, to the broken heart of our God, down to the propitiation for our sins; let us put away the books that have sapped our faith; let us cut off the interests and the companionships that have weighed our lives down to the dust, and looking to Jesus, let us build ourselves up on our most holy faith.

## Praying in the Holy Spirit

That is the next step after laying the foundation of faith. Nothing is so hard as to pray aright. Do *you* pray for God's servants till your heart glows? Do you ask for your minister that he may be set ablaze with divine fire? Do you pray Sunday after Sunday that souls may be converted to God? Have you ever asked for the Holy Spirit?

We can only keep ourselves in the love of God by building up ourselves on our most holy faith and by Holy Spirit-praying, and by nothing else. If we try to fight God's battles with our own weapons, in our own moral-resisting power, we shall fail, and fail miserably; but if we use the spiritual weapons of implicit trust in God, a simple relationship to Jesus Christ, and prayer in the Holy Spirit, we shall never fail.

## "Keep Yourselves in the Love of God"

We know how to keep ourselves in health, how to keep ourselves in knowledge, and so on; but to keep ourselves in the love of God is a big order, and our minds are exercised to know what Jude means by this exhortation. Does relaxing all stringency and carefulness mean that we slip out into a broad, humanitarian spirit that says, "God is love," and "God's in his heaven; all's right with the world"? No, it cannot mean anything so natural as that; otherwise we had no need of an inspired writer to tell us to do it. And beside, Jude strikes terrible notes of warning (see vv. 17–19). "Keep yourselves in the love of God" refers very clearly to something distinct and special, something revealed in the direct will of God; a spiritual endeavor that we must consider, and consider carefully, with the Holy Spirit's help.

"Keep" means work. It is not a lazy floating; it is work. Work, or you will depart from the love of God. Begin to trace the finger of God and the love of God in the great calamities of earth, and in the calamities that have befallen you. In sweat of brain and spirit, work—agonizing at times—to keep yourself in the love of God. It is our wisdom, our happiness, our security to keep ourselves in the love of God.

How do I keep myself in any sphere but by using every means to abide in it? If I wish to keep in the spiritual sphere of the love of God I must use the great organ of the spiritual realm, faith. "God loves me." Say it over and over and over, heedless of your feelings that come and go. Do not live at a distance from God; live near Him, delighting yourself in Him. Remove all barriers of selfishness and fear, and plunge into the fathomless love of God.

"Keep yourselves in the love of God," not "keep on loving God." None can do that. When once you have understood the truth about your own heart's sinfulness, think not again of it, but look at the great, vast, illimitable magnificence of the love of God. Oh, may we be driven—driven further and further out into the ocean fullness of the love of God, taking care that nothing entices us out of that fullness again.

"Who shall separate us from the love of Christ?" Oh, the fullness of peace and joy and gladness when we are persuaded that nothing "shall be able to separate us from the love of God, which is in Christ Jesus our Lord" (Romans 8:35, 38–39).

# If God Is Love—Why?

It is easy to say "God is love" when there is no war and when everything is going well; but it is not so easy to say when everything that happens actually gives the lie to it. For instance, when a person realizes he has an incurable disease, or a severe handicap in life, or when all that is dear has been taken from him, to be able to say, facing these things, "God is love," means he has got hold of something the average person has missed.

Love is difficult to define, but the working definition I would like to give is that "Love is the sovereign preference of my person for another person, embracing everyone and everything in that preference."

Run your idea for all it is worth. When we are young we think things are simpler than they are; we have an idea for every domain. A person says he is a materialist, or an agnostic, or a Christian, meaning he has only one main idea, but very few will run that idea for all it is worth. Yet this is the only way to discover whether it will work, and the same thing is true in the idea of the Christian religion that God is love.

## Nature of God's Love

But God demonstrates His own love toward us, in that while we were still sinners, Christ died for us. (Romans 5:8)

The love of God is different from the love of everyone else. "God demonstrates His *own* love toward us." It is not like the love of a father or mother, or a wife or lover. It is of such a peculiar stamp that it has to be demonstrated to us; we do not believe God's love.

**The foundation of God's love** is holiness—"without which no one will see the Lord." (Hebrews 12:14). God's love then must be the justification of His holiness. Remember our definition—love is the sovereign preference of my person for another person, embracing everyone and everything in that preference. If God's nature is holy, His love must be holy love, seeking to embrace everyone and everything until we all become holy.

**The features of God's love**—that is, the way His love as revealed in the Bible manifests itself in common life—are unfamiliar to us. The average commonsense man is completely puzzled by such a verse as John 3:16. The revelation of Christianity has to do with the foundation of things, not primarily with actual life, and when the gospel is proclaimed it is proclaimed as the foundation. A feature of God's love is that if we will commit ourselves to Him, He will impart to us the very nature of His Son. "The gift of God is eternal life" (Romans 6:23, italics added).

**The fact of God's love:** "God was in Christ reconciling the world to Himself" (2 Corinthians 5:19). These are subjects that have no weight with us in our ordinary way of looking at things. They do not live in the same street because they are not in the street, but in the foundation of things. When war or some other calamity hits us hard and knocks us out of the commonplace, we are prepared to listen to what the Bible has to say, and we discover the Bible deals with the foundation of things that lie behind our common-sense life. The Bible does not deal with the domain of common-sense facts; we get at those by our senses. The Bible deals with the world of revelation, facts which we only get at by faith in God.

## Nature and God's Love

For the earnest expectation of the creation eagerly waits for the revealing of the sons of God. (Romans 8:19)

Does nature exhibit the creator as a God of love? If so, why is nature a scene of plunder and murder? Has the Bible anything to say about it, any revelation that explains it? Try and weave a concept of God out of Jesus Christ's presentation of Him and then look at life as it is, and you will find that God, as He is revealed in Jesus Christ, is flatly contradicted in the natural world. God is the only Being who can afford to be misunderstood; He deliberately stands aside and lets Himself be slandered and misrepresented; He never vindicates Himself.

When we touch the cosmic force apart from the "blinkers" of intellect, there is a wild problem in it. Nature is wild, not tame. Modern science would have us believe it is tame—that we can harness the sea and the air. Quite true, if we only read scientific manuals and deal with successful experiments; but after a while we discover that there are elements that knock men's calculations on the head and prove that the universe is wild and unmanageable. Yet God in the beginning created man to have dominion over it. The reason he cannot is that he has twisted the order and become master of himself, instead of recognizing God's dominion over him. Jesus Christ belonged to the order of things God originally intended for mankind. He was easily Master of the life of the sea and air and earth. If we want to know what the human race will be like on the basis of redemption, we shall find it mirrored in Jesus Christ, a perfect oneness between God and man. In the meantime there is a gap, and the universe is wild. Paul says that creation is out of gear and twisted, that it is waiting for the manifestation of the sons of God. The New Testament view of nature is that it is subject to bondage, that it is in a disorganized condition, out of gear with God's purpose; it is twisted and will only be right when God and man are again one (see Romans 8).

God is responsible for the established order of nature, so if God created nature and we have not the Spirit of God, we shall never interpret the order of nature as God does.

**The indifference of nature:** "Thorns and thistles it shall bring forth for you, and you shall eat the herb of the field. In the sweat of your face you shall eat bread, till you return to the ground . . . (Genesis 3:18–19). This needs an explanation no man can reach by common sense. The Bible says that nature is indifferent because it became disorganized through the disobedience of the human race. The indifference of nature hits us sorely when our hearts are stirred by bereavement—the inscrutable sadness of nature on the human spirit. The early mornings, the late nights, seascapes and mountain scenes, awaken in the sensitive human spirit not in touch with God an ineffable sadness, ages weary, ages sad, ages worn out, pointing to this very fact that God is amazingly remote from man because man has externalized himself.

**The iniquity of nature:** "Now I saw a new heaven and a new earth, for the first heaven and the first earth had passed away. Also there was no more sea" (Revelation 21:1). There is nothing more cruel than the sun or more blasting than the desert. There is an element of twisted spite in the sea in certain aspects of human life. A sailor's wife, for instance, has reason to have a deep fear and hatred of the sea. In the jungles of vast continents the most cruel and unspeakable horrors take place. These are some things that make it the height of impertinence to say glibly, "God is love."

**The infidelity of nature:** "The wolf also shall dwell with the lamb . . . They shall not hurt nor destroy in all My holy mountain, for the earth shall be full of the knowledge of the LORD, as the waters cover the sea" (Isaiah 11:6, 9). Isaiah is speaking of a time when all the indifference and iniquity and infidelity of nature will be gone, when "the wolf shall dwell with the lamb"—a relationship will exist which now is inconceivable; at present the lamb lies down inside the wolf! Earth is man's domain, but the Bible talks about a "hereafter" without the sin and iniquity—"a new heaven and a new earth." We are going to be here, marvelously redeemed, in this wonderful place that God made very beautiful, in which sin has played havoc.

## Nations and God's Love

The kingdoms of this world have become the kingdoms of our Lord and of his Christ, and He shall reign forever and ever. (Revelation 11:15)

We talk about a Christian nation—there never has been such a thing. There are Christians in the nations, but not Christian nations. The constitution of a nation is the same as that of a human being. There is a difference between individuality and personality. Individuality is all elbows and must stand alone; personality is something that can be merged and blended. Individuality is the husk of the personal life; when personal life is emancipated, individuality goes. So with nations. The kingdoms of this world have become intensely individualistic, with no love for God or care for one another. The insistence of nations is that they must keep the national peace—in the way they have been doing it! In the whirlwind of nations, such as is on just now, many have lost—not their faith in God (I never met anyone who lost his faith in God), but their belief in their beliefs, and for a while they think they have lost their faith in God. They have lost the concept that has been presented to them as God, and are coming to God on a new line.

**The origin of nations:** "Now the whole earth had one language and one speech . . . Therefore its name is called Babel, because there the LORD confused the language of all the earth; and from there the LORD scattered them abroad over the face of all the earth" (Genesis 11:1, 9). According to the Bible, nations as we know them are the outcome of what ought never to have been. Civilization was founded on murder, and the basis of our civilized life is competition. There are grand ingredients in civilization—it is full of shelter and protection—but its basis is not good. We each belong to a nation, and each nation imagines that God is an almighty representative of that nation. If nations are right, which is the right one?

**The object of nations:** "Where do wars and fights come from among you? . . . You fight and war. Yet you do not have because you do not ask" (James 4:1–2). The question is on the lips of people today: "Is war of the devil or of God?" It is of neither. It is of men, though both God and the devil are behind it. War is a conflict of wills, either in individuals or in nations. As sure as there is will versus will, there must be punch versus punch. This is the object of nations. They will assert their rule and independence and refuse to be downtrodden. If we cannot by diplomacy make our wills bear on other people, then the last resort is war, and always will be until Jesus Christ brings in His kingdom.

There is one thing worse than war and that is sin. The thing that startles us is not the thing that startles God. We are scared and terrorized when our social order is broken, when thousands of men are killed. Well we may be, but how many of us in times of peace and civilization bother one iota about the state of men's hearts toward God? Yet that is the thing that produces pain in the heart of God—not the wars and devastations that so upset us.

**The obliteration of nations:** "And there were loud voices in heaven, saying, 'The kingdoms of this world have become the kingdoms of our Lord and of His Christ; and He shall reign forever and ever'" (Revelation 11:15). In these last days there is an idea that we are going to dominate everything by a perfect brotherhood. Any mind that expresses its view of the future says we are heading up into a federation of religions and nations where distinctions will be obliterated and there will be a great and universal brotherhood. The quarrels of nations make men look forward to the time when nations will be federated out of independent existence. That is a revolt that is a mental safety valve only. Peter says God is "longsuffering toward us" (2 Peter 3:9). At present He is giving men opportunity to try every line they like in individual life as well as in the life of the nations at large. Some things have not been tried yet, and if God were to cut us off short we would say, "If You had left us a bit longer we could have realized our ideal of society and national life." God is allowing us to prove to the hilt that it cannot be done in any way other than that which Jesus Christ said: that is, by a personal relationship to God through Jesus Christ who is God and Man—One. When sooner or later we come to the end of our tether, we hear Jesus Christ say: "Blessed are the poor in spirit" (Matthew 5:3). If you ask God, He will give you the Holy Spirit, an unsullied heredity through Jesus Christ.

That is how the love of God comes in; and it has to be such a long way round because He is "bringing many sons to glory,"—not mechanisms, but men, full-orbed and sensible all through. Jesus Christ never used a revival meeting to take a person off his guard and then say, "Believe in Me." He always puts the case directly. He even seemed to spurn men when they wanted to follow Him (see Luke 9:57–62). "Another convert to My cause"? Not a bit. "Take time and consider what you are doing. Are you ready to hear what I have to say?"

The love of God is going to embrace everyone and everything in the sovereign preference of His person, which is for His Son. God purposes that every one of us shall partake of the very essential nature of Jesus Christ and stand in complete union with Himself, even as Jesus did. Faith in God is a terrific venture in the dark; we have to believe that God is love in spite of all that contradicts it. Every soul represents some kind of battlefield. The great point for the Christian is to remain perfectly confident in God.

Paul says that when the sons of God are manifested, and everything is in a right relationship with God and expressed in devotion to Jesus Christ, all the wildness and contradiction in nature and in nations will cease, and the love of God will be the great reality.

# THE
# MINISTRY
## OF THE
# UNNOTICED

# THE MINISTRY OF THE UNNOTICED

I will be like the dew to Israel; He shall grow like the lily.
(Hosea 14:5)

The New Testament notices things that from our standpoint do not seem to count. For instance, our Lord called only twelve disciples, but what about all those other disciples of His who were not specially called? The twelve disciples were called for a special purpose; but there were hundreds who followed Jesus and were sincere believers in Him who were unnoticed. We are apt to have a disproportionate view of a Christian because we look only at the exceptions. The exceptions stand out *as* exceptions. The extraordinary conversions and phenomenal experiences are magnificent specimen studies of what happens in the life of everyone, but not one in a million has an experience such as the apostle Paul had.

The majority of us are unnoticed and unnoticeable people. If we take the extraordinary experience as a model for the Christian life, we erect a wrong standard without knowing it, and in the passing of the years we produce the spiritual prig—an intolerant unlikeness to Jesus Christ. The man or woman who becomes a spiritual prig does so by imperceptible degrees, but the starting-point is a departure from the gospel of the New Testament and a building up on the evangel of Protestantism.

## The Unaffected Loveliness of the Commonplace

Blessed are the poor in spirit. (Matthew 5:3)

Literally, "Blessed are the paupers in spirit." A pauper is exceedingly commonplace. The average type of preaching emphasizes strength of will and beauty of character—the things that can be easily noticed. The phrase "decide for Christ," which we so frequently hear, is too often an emphasis on the thing our Lord never trusted. Our Lord never asks us to *decide for Him*. He asks us to *yield to Him*—a very different matter.

At the basis of our Lord's kingdom is this unaffected loveliness of the commonplace. The thing in which I am blessed is my poverty. If I know I have no strength of will, no nobility of disposition, then, says Jesus, "Blessed are you," because it is through that poverty that I enter into the kingdom of heaven. I cannot enter the kingdom of heaven as a good man or woman; I can only enter the kingdom of heaven as a complete pauper.

**The influence of disadvantage:** "Like a lily among thorns, so is my love among the daughters" (Song of Solomon 2:2). The lily Solomon refers to is as common as our daisy, but a perfume pervades it. The illustration is as if a traveler were passing a field and suddenly a fragrant aroma was wafted to him from a bush. Marveling at the sweetness, he looked into the bush and found a lily growing in its bosom. People come to a good but worldly home and say, "What a beautiful influence comes from that home!" But begin to draw aside the ordinary commonplace things of the home, and you discover that tucked away somewhere is a mother or a daughter who is really a "lily" of the Lord. Or take it in connection with individual lives. We may see a man who is generally disadvantaged in appearance or in education, a thoroughly commonplace man, yet a marvelous influence radiates from him. Our Lord is spoken of as "a root out of a dry ground"—thoroughly disadvantaged. That is what Isaiah says the hero of God will be like.

The true character of the loveliness that tells for God is always unconscious. Conscious influence is priggish and un-Christian. When we begin to wonder whether we are of any use, we instantly lose the bloom of the touch of the Lord. Jesus says, "He who believes in Me . . . out of his heart will flow rivers of living water" (John 7:38). If we begin to examine outflow, we lose touch with the source. We have to pay attention to the source and God will look after the outflow.

The same thing is true with regard to the "passion for souls," the great craze for successful service. Our Lord told the disciples not to rejoice in successful service, but to rejoice because they were rightly related to Him (see Luke 10:18–20). The danger in all these things is that we are apt to make the effect the cause. Who are the people who have influenced us most? Certainly not the priggish men and women, but our mothers, our fathers, our sisters—the ones who had not the remotest idea that they were influencing us.

**The inspiration of detail:** "The capitals which were on top of the pillars in the hall were in the shape of lilies" (1 Kings 7:19) The decorative lilies added nothing to the strength of the building. Many would notice the strength and the majesty of the whole building, but the inspiration of it all was in the detail, in "the shape of lilies."

In architecture it is not so much the massive strength that counts as the finely proportioned ornament, and that is never obtrusive. If we look at men and women who have been long at work for God and have been going through chastening, we notice that they have lost their individual harshness, lost a great deal of their apparent go-aheadness for God; but they have acquired something else, namely, the exquisite "shape of lilies" in their lives, and this after all is the thing most like Jesus Christ. It is the quiet, undisturbable divinity that is characteristic of Jesus, not aggressiveness, and the same is true of God's children. This does not mean that our Lord is not aggressive, or that God's children are not aggressive, but it does mean that there is a danger of making so much of the aggressive that we neglect the more important aspect—the ministry of the unnoticed.

God will use any number of extraordinary things to chisel the detail of His "shape of lilies" in His children. He will use people who are like hedgehogs; He will use difficult circumstances like the weather; He will use anything and everything, no matter what it is, and we shall always know when God is at work because He produces in the commonplace something that is inspiring.

**The implicitness of distinction:** "Consider the lilies . . ." (Matthew 6:28). When our Lord described the spiritual life, He always took His illustrations from His Father's handiwork, never from man's work. We take our illustrations from automobiles or airplanes, or electricity, or something go-ahead and self-advertising. We illustrate by means of things that compel our attention, but Jesus mentions things we are not compelled to look at, things we would pass by. How many of us notice sparrows and daisies and grass? They are so plentiful that we ignore them, yet it is these things Jesus tells us to consider. The characteristic of each of these things is implicitness, not explicitness.

Imagine a lily, if it could speak, saying, "I am going to be a lily!" A lily obeys the law of its life where it is placed. It is unconscious in its growth. In Isaiah 47:7, we read: "And you said, 'I shall be a lady forever.'" The characteristic of a lady is implicitness, not explicitness, and in the same way a Christian is one in whom the indwelling Spirit of God shines out all the time. In the Christian life the implicit is never conscious; if it becomes conscious, it ceases to have the unaffected loveliness that is the characteristic of the life of Jesus Christ. Prudery is the outcome of obedience to a principle, whereas, according to our Lord, purity is the outcome of an implicit relationship. If we look upon purity as the outcome of obedience to a particular standard, we produce the opposite of what our Lord intends. He said, "Unless you . . . become as little children . . ." (Matthew 18:3, italics added).

## The Unconscious Light in Circumstances

If I then, your Lord and Teacher, have washed your feet, you also ought to wash one another's feet. (John 13:14)

What were the circumstances here? A supper table, a dozen fishermen, a basin of water, a towel, and our Lord washing the feet of the fishermen. Notice the extraordinary sequence of this event. "Jesus, knowing that the Father had given all things into His hands, and that He had come from God and was going to God . . ." (John 13:3). Had the Transfiguration scene followed this, we would have felt it to be the right order. But instead, "He rose from supper and laid aside His garments, took a towel and girded Himself. After that He poured water into a basin and began to wash the disciples' feet" (John 13:4–5). Could anything be more sordid and commonplace? But it takes God incarnate to do the most menial task properly. We may often use a towel to exhibit a characteristic totally unlike Jesus Christ. Whatever our Lord touched became wonderful. Some people do a certain thing and the way in which they do it hallows that thing to us forever afterward. When our Lord does anything, He always transfigures it.

Notice the words that our Lord glorified. A word that was

scorned when He came was the word *servant*, yet Jesus said: "I am among you as the One who serves" (Luke 22:27), and, "whoever of you desires to be first shall be slave of all" (Mark 10:44). Our Lord took words that were despised and transfigured their meaning; He did things that were commonplace and sordid and ordinary and transfigured them. Our Lord was the unconscious light in the most ordinary circumstances conceivable.

Many who knew our Lord while He was on earth saw nothing in Him; only after their disposition had been altered did they realize who He was. Christ lived so ordinary a life that no one noticed Him. The disciples were first attracted to Jesus by their sense of the heroic and the holy, but it was not until they had received the Holy Spirit that "their eyes were opened, and they knew Him" (Luke 24:31). Could anything more startling be imagined than for someone to point out a Nazarene carpenter and say, "That man is God Incarnate"? It would sound blasphemous to a Pharisee.

Our Lord did not say to His disciples: "I have had a most successful time on earth; I have addressed thousands of people and been the means of their salvation. Now you go and do the same kind of thing." He said: "If I then, your Lord and Teacher, have washed your feet, *you also ought to wash one another's feet*" (John 13:14, italics added). We try to get out of it by washing the feet of those who are not of our own set. We will wash the heathen's feet, the feet in the slums; but fancy washing my brother's feet! my wife's! my husband's! the feet of the minister of my church! Our Lord said *"one another's feet."* It is in the ordinary commonplace circumstances that the unconscious light of God is seen.

**The trackless waste:** "You are the light of the world" (Matthew 5:14). In the New Testament "world" means the system of things that has been built on God's earth, the system of religion or of society or of civilization that never takes Jesus Christ into account. Jesus said we are to be the light there. We need to take on us the pattern and print of Jesus Christ, not the pattern and print of the world, and immediately when we try to be what Jesus wants us to be, we shall find the truth of what He said: they shall "revile you and cast out your name as evil" (Luke 6:22). The "camp" to which we belong will do it, not the world. It is easier to remain true to our camp than to Jesus, easier to be loyal to our convictions than to Him.

"You are the light of the world." We have the idea that we are going to shine in heaven, but we are to shine down here, "in the midst of a crooked and perverse generation" (Philippians 2:15). We are to shine as lights in the world in the squalid places, and it cannot be done by putting on a brazen smile. The light must be there all the time.

"You are the light of the world." We ourselves are to be the light wherever we go; but if ever we became conscious of it, we should be amazed, as Mary of Bethany must have been amazed at Jesus Christ's interpretation of her act of devotion. Mary simply discharged her overburdened heart in a demonstration of affection for Jesus Christ, and He said that "wherever this gospel be preached in the whole world, what this woman has done will also be told as a memorial to her" (Mark 14:9).

**The trifling ways:** "It gives light to all who are in the house" (Matthew 5:15). The light is to be shown in all the trifling ways of home life. The average evangelical presentation is apt to produce a contempt for the trifling ways. A preacher of the gospel may be a most objectionable being at home instead of giving light in the ordinary ways. Our Lord tells us to judge the preacher or the teacher "by his fruits." Fruit is not the salvation of souls, that is God's work. Fruit is "the fruit of the Spirit"—love, joy, peace, and all the rest. We get much more concerned about not offending other people than about offending our Lord. Jesus Christ often offended people, but He never put a stumbling block in anyone's way.

**The truthful witness:** " . . . that they may see your good works" (Matthew 5:16). Our Lord did not say "that you may preach the right thing." It is an easy business to preach—an appallingly easy thing to tell other people what to do. It is another thing to have God's message turned into a boomerang. "You have been teaching these people that they should be full of peace and of joy, but what about yourself? Are you full of peace and joy?" The truthful witness is the one who lets his light shine in works that exhibit the disposition of Jesus; one who lives the truth as well as preaches it.

## The Unadvertised Life for the Community

And we also ought to lay down our lives for the brethren.
(1 John 3:16)

A mother lays down her life for her child and for her home, but she does not advertise what she is doing. The child will never recognize what the mother has done until in years to come the child is in the same place. Only then will the unadvertised substitution of the mother's life and love be recognized.

This is what Jesus Christ has done in His redemptive work. "By this we know love, because He laid down His life for us. And we also ought to lay down our lives for the brethren" (1 John 3:16). Jesus Christ was made broken bread and poured-out wine for us, and He expects us to be made broken bread and poured-out wine in His hands for others. If we are not thoroughly baked, we will produce indigestion because we are dough instead of bread. We have to be made into good nutritious stuff for other people. The reason we are going through the things we are is that God wants to know whether He can make us good bread with which to feed others. The stuff of our lives, not simply of our talk, is to be the nutriment of those who know us.

**The submissive days:** "Then He went down with them . . . and was subject to them" (Luke 2:51). An extraordinary exhibition of submissiveness! And "the disciple is not above his master." Think of it: thirty years at home with brothers and sisters who did not believe in Him! We fix on the three years that were extraordinary in our Lord's life and forget altogether the earlier years at home—thirty years of absolute submission. Perhaps something of the same kind is happening to you, and you say, "I don't know why I should have to submit to this." Are you any better than Jesus Christ? "As He is, so are we in this world" (1 John 4:17). The explanation of it all is our Lord's prayer—"that they may be one as We are" (John 17:11). If God is putting you through a spell of submission and you seem to be losing your individuality and everything else, it is because Jesus is making you one with Him.

**The solitary desertions:** "And He was there in the wilderness forty days, tempted by Satan, and was with the wild beasts . . . " (Mark 1:13). The divine, the desert, the devil, and utter desolation "with the wild beasts." If our Lord endured solitary desolation, why should we consider it strange when we are solitary and without comradeship? Thank God we have a solitary life. It is in the solitary life that we prove whether we are willing to be made the unadvertised life for the community to which we belong—whether we are willing to be made bread or to be simply the advertisement for bread. If we are to be made bread, then we must not be surprised if we are treated in the way our Lord was treated.

**The substitution devotion:** "Greater love has no one than this, than to lay down one's life for his friends. You are My friends if you do whatever I command you" (John 15:13–14). For a man to lay down his life is not to lay it down in a sudden crisis, such as death, but to lay it down in deliberate expenditure as one would lay out a pound note. Not—"Here it is. Take it out in one huge martyrdom and be done with it." It is a continual substitution whereby we realize that we have another day to spend for Jesus Christ, another opportunity to prove ourselves His friends.

# CAN YOU COME DOWN?

Now after six days Jesus took Peter, James, and John, and led them up on a high mountain apart by themselves; and He was transfigured before them. His clothes became shining, exceedingly white, like snow, such as no launderer on earth can whiten them. And Elijah appeared to them with Moses, and they were talking with Jesus.

Then Peter answered and said to Jesus, "Rabbi, it is good for us to be here; and let us make three tabernacles: one for You, one for Moses, and one for Elijah" because he did not know what to say, for they were greatly afraid.

And a cloud came and overshadowed them; and a voice came out of the cloud, saying, "This is My beloved Son. Hear Him!" Suddenly, when they had looked around, they saw no one anymore, but only Jesus with themselves. Now as they came down from the mountain, He commanded them that they should tell no one the things they had seen, till the Son of Man had risen from the dead. So they kept this word to themselves, questioning what the rising from the dead meant.

And they asked Him, saying, "Why do the scribes say that Elijah must come first?"

Then He answered and told them, "Indeed, Elijah is coming first and restores all things. And how is it written concerning the Son of Man, that He must suffer many things and be treated with contempt? But I say to you that Elijah has also come, and they did to him whatever they wished, as it is written of him."

And when He came to the disciples, He saw a great multitude around them, and scribes disputing with them. Immediately, when they saw Him, all the people were greatly amazed, and running to *Him*, greeted Him. And He asked the scribes, "What are you discussing with them?"

Then one of the crowd answered and said, "Teacher, I brought You my son, who has a mute spirit. And wherever it seizes him, it throws him down; he foams at the mouth, gnashes his teeth, and becomes rigid. So I spoke to Your disciples, that they should cast it out, but they could not."

He answered him and said, "O faithless generation, how long shall I be with you? How long shall I bear with you? Bring him to Me."

Then they brought him to Him. And when he saw Him, immediately the spirit convulsed him, and he fell on the ground and wallowed, foaming at the mouth. So He asked his father, "How long has this been happening to him?" And he said, "From childhood. And often he has thrown him both into the fire and into the water to destroy him. But if You can do anything, have compassion on us and help us."

Jesus said to him, "If you can believe, all things *are* possible to him who believes."

Immediately the father of the child cried out and said with tears, "Lord, I believe; help my unbelief!"

When Jesus saw that the people came running together, He rebuked the unclean spirit, saying to it, "Deaf and dumb spirit, I command you, come out of him and enter him no more!"

Then *the spirit* cried out, convulsed him greatly, and came out of him. And he became as one dead, so that many said, "He is dead." But Jesus took him by the hand and lifted him up, and he arose.

And when He had come into the house, His disciples asked Him privately, "Why could we not cast it out?"

So He said to them, "This kind can come out by nothing but prayer and fasting." (Mark 9:2–29)

The test of spiritual life is the power to descend; if we have power to rise only, there is something wrong. We all have had times on the mount when we have seen things from God's standpoint and we wanted to stay there; but if we are disciples of Jesus Christ, He will never allow us to stay there. Spiritual selfishness makes us want to stay on the mount. We feel so good, as if we could do anything—talk like angels and live like angels, if only we could stay there. But there must be the power to descend. The mountain is not the place for us to live; we were built for the valleys. This is one of the hardest things to learn, because spiritual selfishness always wants repeated moments on the mount.

## The Sphere of Exaltation

Then Peter answered and said to Jesus, "Rabbi, it is good for us to be here; and let us make three tabernacles: one for You, one for Moses, and one for Elijah. (Mark 9:5)

When God gives us a time of exaltation it is always exceptional. It has its meaning in our life with God, but we must beware lest spiritual selfishness wants to make it the only time. The sphere of exaltation is not meant to teach us anything. We are apt to think that everything that happens to us is to be turned into useful teaching; it is to be turned into something better than teaching, namely, into character. We shall find that the spheres God brings us into are not meant to teach us something but to *make* us something.

There is a great danger in asking, "What is the use of it?" There is no *use* in it at all. If you want a life of usefulness, don't be a Christian after our Lord's stamp; you will be much more useful if you are not. The cry for the standard of usefulness knocks the spiritual Christian right out; he dare not touch it if he is going to remain true to his Master. Take the life of our Lord: for three years all He did was to walk about saying things and healing sick people—a useless life, judged from every standard of success and enterprise. If our Lord and His disciples had lived in our day, they would have been put down as a most unuseful crowd.

In spiritual matters we can never calculate on the line of "What is the use of it?" "What is the use of being at a Bible training college? Of learning psychology and ethics? *Do* something." Great danger lies along that line. "The good is ever the enemy of the best." The mountaintop experiences are rare moments, but they are meant for something in the purposes of God. It was not until Peter came to write his epistles that he realized the full purpose of his having been on the Mount of Transfiguration.

## The Sphere of Humiliation

Then one of the crowd answered and said, "Teacher, I brought You my son, who has a mute spirit. And wherever it seizes him, it throws him down; he foams at the mouth;

gnashes his teeth, and becomes rigid. So I spoke to Your disciples, that they should cast it out, but they could not. (Mark 9:17–18)

The first thing the disciples met in the valley was a demon-possessed boy, and we have to live in the demon-possessed valley. God did not create Adam to live on the mountain; He made him of the dust of the earth—that was his glory.

The mountaintop is an exceptional type of experience. We have to live down in the valley. After every time of exaltation we are brought down with a sudden rush into things as they are, where things are neither beautiful nor poetic nor spiritual nor thrilling. The height of the mountaintop is measured by the drab drudgery of the valley. We never live for the glory of God on the mount. We *see* His glory there, but we do not live for His glory there; it is in the valley that we live for the glory of God. Our Lord came down from the mount into the valley and went on to the cross, where He was glorified. We have to come down from the mount of exaltation into the drab life of the valley.

It is in the sphere of humiliation that we find our true worth to God, and that is where our faithfulness has to be manifested. Most of us can do things if we are always at the heroic pitch; but God wants us at the drab, commonplace pitch, where we live in the valley according to our personal relationship to Him. We can all be thrilled by appeals to do things in an ecstatic way, by moments of devotion, but that is never the work of God's grace; it is the natural selfishness of our own hearts. We can all do the heroic thing, but can we live in the valley where there is nothing amazing, but mostly disaster, certainly humiliation, and emphatically everything drab and dull and common? That is where Jesus Christ lived most of His life. The reason we have to live in the valley is that the majority of people live there, and if we are to be of use to God in the world, we must be useful from God's standpoint—not from our own standpoint or the standpoint of other people.

"But if You can do anything, have compassion on us and help us" (Mark 9:22). That is our condition when we are in the valley. We do not know God; we are full of skepticism. The great point of our life with God and of our service for Him in the world is that we get the skepticism rooted out of us, and it takes the valley of humiliation to root it out. Look back at your own experience and you will find that until you learned who Jesus Christ was, you were a cunning skeptic about His power. When you were on the mount you could believe anything, because it was in accordance with the selfishness of your nature. But what about the time when you were up against facts in the valley, up against questions that could not be answered? You may be perfectly able to give a testimony to sanctification, but what about the thing that is a humiliation to you? If you are without something that is a humiliation to you, I question whether you have ever come into a personal relationship with Jesus Christ.

We are called to fellowship with His sufferings, and some of the greatest suffering lies in remaining powerless where He remained powerless. Had our Lord been a man, He would have healed the boy at first, but He waited until the father was in the last ebb of despair: "If You can do anything, have compassion on us and help us."

Am I patient enough in my faith in Jesus Christ to allow people to get to the last ebb of despair before they see what He can do? We step in in a thousand and one ways God never tells us to; we say we cannot bear to see God appear cruel, but God has to appear cruel from our standpoint. As disciples of Jesus we have to learn not only what our Lord is like on the Mount of Transfiguration, but what He is like in the valley of humiliation, where everything is giving the lie to His power, where the disciples are powerless, and where He is not doing anything.

## The Sphere of Ministration

So He said to them, "This kind can come out by nothing but prayer and fasting. (Mark 9:29)

The last time you were on the mount with God you saw that all power has been given unto Jesus in heaven and on earth. Are you going to be skeptical in the valley of humiliation? Over and over again you have gone to God about the thing that is perplexing you and nothing has happened. "Why could we not  cast it out?" Our Lord never gives an answer to questions of that description, because the answer lies in a personal relationship to Himself. "This kind can come out by nothing but prayer and fasting," that is, by concentration and redoubled concentration on Him. Prayer and fasting means concentration on God. That is the one purpose for which we are in the world.

Do get out of your ears the noisy cries of the Christian world we are in: "Do this and do that." Never! *Be* this and that, then I will do through you," says Jesus. "If You can? Is that what you say to Me? All things are possible to him who believes."

At last the father got to the point of personal relationship with Jesus. "Lord, I believe; help My unbelief." We slander God by our very eagerness to work for Him without knowing Him.

We must be able to mount up with wings as eagles, but we must know also how to come down. It is the coming down and the living down that is the power of the saint. Paul said, "I can do all things through Christ who strengthens me" (Philippians 4:13). Watch the things He said He could do—they were all humiliating things. We have the idea that we are meant to work for God along the heroic line; we are meant to do unheroic work for God in the martyr spirit. The sphere of humiliation is always the place of more satisfaction to Jesus Christ, and it is in our power to refuse to be humiliated. To say, "No, thank you, I much prefer to be on the mountaintop with God."

Do I believe that God engineers my circumstances? That it is He who brings me each day into contact with the people I meet? Am I faithful enough to Him to know that all I meet with every day is absolutely under His dominance and rule? Do I face humiliation with a perfect knowledge that God is working out His own will?

You are brought face to face with difficult cases, and nothing happens externally; yet you know that emancipation has been given, because *you* are concentrated on Jesus Christ. Our line of service is to see that there is nothing between Jesus and ourselves. Is there? If there is, you must get through it, not by mounting up, not by ignoring it in irritation, but by facing it and going through it straight into the presence of Jesus. Then that very thing, and all you have been through in connection with it, glorifies Jesus in a way you will never know till you see Him face to face.

When we look at our lives in this way, we understand what Jesus meant when He said, "He who believes in Me . . . out of his heart will flow rivers of living water" (John 7:38). Why should we ignore what Jesus Christ says? Why should we take our stamp of Christian service from any one other than Himself? We have to maintain our personal relationship to Jesus Christ, keep the attitude of a child, and maintain the same attitude in everything and to everyone— toward every individual and circumstance we meet—and never be deflected. That is the meaning of "prayer and fasting."

# THE DEDICATION OF FOLLOWING

Be ye therefore followers of God as dear children.
(Ephesians 5:1 KJV)

## The Followers of God's Life

The one striking thing about following is we must not find our own way, for when we take the initiative we cease to follow. In the natural world everything depends upon our taking the initiative, but if we are followers of God, we cannot take the initiative. We cannot choose our own work or say what we will do; we have not to find out at all, we have just to follow.

"Jesus said to him, . . . you follow Me" (John 21:22). Everything our Lord asks us to do is naturally impossible to us. It is impossible for us to be the children of God naturally, to love our enemies, to forgive, to be holy, to be pure; and it is certainly impossible for us to follow God naturally. Consequently the fundamental fact to recognize is that we must be born again. We recognize it fundamentally, but we must recognize it actually, that in spiritual matters we must not take the initiative. We must not make decisions of our own; we must "follow the Lamb wherever He goes" (Revelation 14:4), and when He does not go anywhere, then we do not.

In following our Lord Jesus Christ we are not following His followers. When Paul said, "who will remind you of my ways," he was careful to add, "in Christ" (1 Corinthians 4:17). We are not called to follow in all the footsteps of the saints, but only insofar as they followed their Lord. The great meaning of following is that we imitate as children, not as monkeys.

"In Him was life . . ." (John 1:4). We are not left to anything vague. It does sound vague to say "Be followers of God," but when we realize that Jesus Christ is the life of God, then we know where we are. He is the one whom we have to imitate and follow, but we must first of all be born again and receive His Spirit, and then walk in the Spirit. "If anyone does not have the Spirit of Christ, he is not His" (Romans 8:9).

**In joy:** "These things I have spoken to you, that My joy may remain in you, and that your joy may be full" (John 15:11). If Jesus Christ is the life of God and we have to follow Him, we must find out what His joy was. It certainly was not happiness. The joy of the Lord Jesus Christ lay in doing exactly what He came to do. He did not come to save men first of all; He came to do His Father's will. The saving of men was the natural outcome of this, but our Lord's one great obedience was not to the needs of men but to the will of His Father, and He says, "as the Father has sent Me, I also send you" (John 20:21). We are never told to consecrate our gifts to God, but we are told to dedicate ourselves.

The joy of anything, from a blade of grass upward, is to fulfill its created purpose "that we who first trusted in Christ should be to the praise of His glory" (Ephesians 1:12). We are not here to win souls and to do good to others; that is the natural outcome, but it is not our aim, and this is where so many of us cease to be followers. We will follow God as long as He makes us a blessing to others; but when He does not, we will not follow. Suppose our Lord had measured His life by whether or not He was a blessing to others? Why, He was a "stone of stumbling" to thousands, actually to His own neighbors, to His own nation, because through Him they blasphemed the Holy Spirit, and in His own country "He did not do many mighty works there because of their unbelief" (Matthew 13:58). If our Lord had measured His life by its actual results, He would have been full of misery.

We get switched off when instead of following God we follow Christian work and workers. We are much more concerned over the passion for souls than the passion for Christ. The passion for Christ is the counterpart of His passion for God. The life of God is manifested in our Lord Jesus Christ who came to do His Father's will. Thus, when we are following Him, it will be a matter of indifference whether God puts us in the forefront or in the back seat. When we realize this, then the joy of the Lord is ours because we are fulfilling our regenerated purpose. The passion for souls is not a New Testament idea at all, but religious commercialism. When we are taken up with this passion the joy of the Lord is never ours, but only an excitable joy, which always leaves a snare behind.

God engineers our circumstances as He did those of His Son; all we have to do is to follow where He places us. The majority of us are busy trying to place ourselves. God alters things while we wait for Him. Are we fulfilling the purpose of our recreation, namely, to glorify God? The sign that we are glorifying God is not that we are happy; happiness is childish, individual and pagan. It is natural for a child to be happy because a child does not face facts. But a Christian who is merely happy is blind.

The way God's life manifests itself in joy is in a peace that has no desire for praise. When a man delivers a message that he knows is the message of God, the witness to the fulfilment of the created purpose is given instantly. The peace of God settles down, and the man cares for neither praise nor blame from anyone. That is the joy of the life of God; it is uncrushable life, and there is never life without joy.

**In judgment:** "He who does the truth comes to the light" (John 3:21). In actual life we must be always in the light, and we cease to be in the light when we want to explain why we did a thing. The significant thing about our Lord is that He never explained anything because He always lived in the light. There is so much in us that is folded and twisted, but the sign that we are following God is that we keep in the light. "I have been saved and sanctified, therefore I am all right"—that brings darkness at once.

When we are walking in the light there is never any lust of vindication, no saying before God, "I did not mean this," or, "I did not intend to do that," or, "I made a mistake there," but always coming to the light and keeping in the light all the time, with nothing folded before God. We keep in the judgment of God, consequently there is no condemnation going on in our lives. "There is therefore now no condemnation to those who are in Christ Jesus" (Romans 8:1) means keeping in the light all the time.

One danger is to go off in work, and another danger is to go off on doctrine. Doctrine is the mere statement of the life of God for the purposes of teaching. Always beware of following your own convictions in doctrine instead of following the life of God. Our Lord says, "Judge not," and yet Paul says that "we shall judge angels." Our Lord means: Do not judge by ordinary reasoning or weighing up by carnal suspicion, but keep in the light. By keeping in the light we judge even angels. It is done by following God's life in judgment.

**In Jerusalem:** "Behold, we are going up to Jerusalem . . . "(Luke 18:31). Jerusalem was the place in the life of our Lord where He actually fulfilled the climax of His Father's will. He did not stay long in the villages where the people were blessed abundantly, He went steadily through everything; successful service or shame, it never affected Him, and we have to do the same. We have to fulfil the purpose of God in our lives. We are here to be followers of the life of God. The counterpart is taking God's life for ourselves instead of giving ourselves to God. If we say, "I want God's life for my body," at once we are off the track. Our bodies are to be entirely at God's disposal, and not God at our disposal. God does give divine health, but not in order to show what a wonderful being a divinely healed person is. The life of God has to be followed by us, not utilized; we must not allow the life of God to stagnate in us, or imagine that we are to be put as specimens in a showcase. If God has healed us and keeps us in health, it is not that we might parade it, but that we might follow the life of God for His purposes.

We do not know where our "Jerusalem" is, but we have to go up to it, and the only way to go up to it is not by trying to find out where it is, but by being followers of God's life.

## The Followers of God's Love

> For I am persuaded, that neither death nor life, nor angels nor principalities nor powers, nor things present nor things to come, nor height nor depth, nor any other created thing, shall be able to separate us from the love of God which is in Christ Jesus our Lord. (Romans 8:38–39)

Jesus Christ is the love of God incarnated. The love of God is not to be looked for in justice, right, truth, and purity. The love of God *is* Jesus Christ.

**In loyalty:** "Stand fast therefore in the liberty by which Christ has made us free, and do not be entangled again with a yoke of bondage" (Galatians 5:1). Loyalty is not to be to loving God or to the love of God, but to Jesus Christ's redemption of us. "Therefore put to death your members which are on the earth: fornication, uncleanness, passion, evil desire, and covetousness, which is idolatry" (Colossians 3:5). "Since I have been saved and sanctified none of these things dwell in me." These things are only possible in the saint, because the saint's body is the temple of the Holy Spirit and may be utilized as an occasion to the flesh. Saints have to become absolutely loyal to the disposition of Jesus Christ in their lives. To "put to death" means to destroy by neglect. It is easy to detect whenever inordinacy comes in. "How then can I do this great wickedness?" (Genesis 39:9). God's love restrained him—that is Joseph's meaning.

The only way to keep following the love of God is by being loyal to the Lord Jesus Christ. If we make sin a theological question and not a question of actual deliverance, we become adherents to doctrine. And if we put doctrine first, we shall be hoodwinked before we know where we are. If we take an actual experience and deposit that as a truth on which we rest our souls, we go wrong at once. In stating holiness doctrinally we are apt to make it appear harsh and vindictive; it is technically right, but without the love of God in it. Paul's phrase, "the holiness of truth," is the right one.

**In liberty:** "Therefore if the Son makes you free, you shall be free indeed" (John 8:36). "Free indeed"—that is, free from the inside. The freedom of Jesus is never license; it is always liberty, and liberty means ability to fulfil the law of God. The law of God was fulfilled in the life of Jesus Christ; therefore He is the expression of the love of God. If I am following God's love as exhibited in the Lord Jesus Christ and He has made me free from within, I am so taken up with following Him that I will never take advantage of another child of God.

**In lowliness:** "But made Himself of no reputation, taking the form of a bondservant, and carrying the likeness of men (Philippians 2:7). In following God's love we must do so in lowliness. "Let this mind be in you which was also in Christ Jesus" (Philippians 2:5).

That is a command. God does not give us the mind of Christ; He gives us the Spirit of Christ, and we have to see that the Spirit of Christ in us works through our brains in contact with actual life and that we form His mind. Jesus Christ did not become humbled; "He humbled Himself" (Philippians 2:8). He was "in the form of God," yet He took on Himself "the form of a bondservant" (Philippians 2:6–7). Some of us make a virtue of modesty and it becomes the worst form of pride. Self-assertive initiative has nothing to do with the love of God, and was never exhibited in the life of Jesus Christ.

We are all thrilled by high, human, noble sacrifice; it is much more thrilling than Calvary. But there is something shameful about that. It is against all human ideas of nobility. The love of God is not in accordance with human standards in any way.

## The Followers of the Lamb

> These are the ones who follow the Lamb wherever He goes. (Revelation 14:4)

**In purity:** "And everyone who has this hope in Him purifies himself, just as He is pure" (1 John 3:3). We are to follow Jesus Christ down here in the actual world where there is any amount of impurity, but we have this hope, that "we shall be like Him;" consequently we purify ourselves. The possibility of being impure means that there is some value to Jesus Christ in our being pure. God gives us His supernatural life, but we have to keep entirely free from the world with a purity that is of value to God; we have to grow in purity. Unless a man realizes that when he is indwelt by the Spirit of God he must also walk according to the pattern of Jesus Christ, his flesh will take occasion to ensnare him. One of the most besmirching impurities lies in money matters. Do we follow the Lamb in these matters? If we do, we shall purify ourselves "just as

He is pure." Not only is the purity of the Holy Spirit in us, but we are working it out in every detail. We have to be God's workmanship, not to work for God. "But you shall receive power when the Holy Spirit has come upon you: and you shall be witnesses to Me" (Acts 1:8)—that is, "those in whom I am delighted."

If Jesus Christ were manifested now, would we be like Him? Or would we have a hundred and one things to do before we could be as He is? We have not been taking time to purify ourselves as He is pure because we have been restless and annoyed; we have imagined that we have things to do that no one can do but ourselves. It may be true, but immediately we think it, we lose out. There is only one lodestar to the saint, the Lord Jesus Christ. We have no business to get into circumstances God does not put us into. Faith means keeping absolutely right with God. He does all the rest. We are only what we are in the dark; all the rest is reputation. What God looks at is what we are in the dark—the imaginations of our minds; the thoughts of our heart; the habits of our bodies; these are the things that mark us in God's sight.

**In patience:** "Because thou hast kept the word of My patience" (Revelation 3:10 KJV). Patience has the meaning of testing—a thing drawn out and tested, drawn out to the last strand in a strain without breaking, and ending in sheer joy. The strain on a violin string when stretched to the uttermost gives it its strength; and the stronger the strain, the finer the sound of our life for God, and He never strains more than we are able to bear. We say, "sorrow, disaster, calamity"; God says, "chastening," and it sounds sweet to Him though it is a discord in our ears. Don't faint when you are rebuked, and don't despise the chastenings of the Lord. "In your patience possess ye your souls" (Luke 21:19 KJV). If God has given you a time of rest, then lie curled up in His leaves of healing.

**In power:** "For though He was crucified in weakness, yet He lives by the power of God. For we also are weak in Him, but we shall live

with Him by the power of God toward you" (2 Corinthians 13:4).
The power of God was exhibited in Jesus Christ—that insignificant Nazarene carpenter whom Roman paganism did not notice.
In the eyes of the world, pagan virtues are admirable; Christian
virtues are contemptible. Are we prepared to be "weak in Him"? If
so, we shall be weaklings in the eyes of men, but we shall "live with
Him by the power of God."

Do we "follow the Lamb wherever He goes"? He will take us
through darkness, through the valley of the shadow, through the
strange dark things. We must follow Him "wherever He goes."

For the Lamb who is in the midst of the throne will shepherd them and lead them to living fountains of waters. And
God will wipe away every tear from their eyes. (Revelation
7:17)

# INVINCIBLE
# CONSOLATION

In loving memory of
Kathleen Mary Cheal Clarke
From God 27th December, 1924
To God 29th September, 1930

Father lead me day by day,
Ever in Thine own sweet way;
Teach me to be good and true,
Show me what I ought to do.

(Kathleen's daily prayer)


Again I shall behold thee, daughter true;
The hour will come when I shall hold thee fast
In God's name, loving thee all through and through.
Somewhere in His grand thought this waits for us.
Then shall I see a smile not like thy last—
For that great thing which came when all was past,
Was not a smile, but God's peace glorious.

—George MacDonald

# INVINCIBLE CONSOLATION

Therefore we do not lose heart. Even though our outward man is perishing, yet the inward man is being renewed day by day. For our light affliction, which is but for a moment, is working for us a far more exceeding and eternal weight of glory, while we do not look at the things which are seen, but at the things which are not seen. For the things which are seen are temporary; but the things which are not seen are eternal. (2 Corinthians 4:16–18)

In these verses the apostle Paul is interpreting the most sacred realities of a saint's life. We deal so much with the joyful and the happy and the exuberant in our experience that we are apt to forget that life externally is continually full of the things Paul mentions here. Paul's own life was one of the most distracting and tumultuous and terribly "spilt" lives ever recorded in history.

## The Beyond Within

**Wasting outward man—Winged inner man:** "Therefore we do not lose heart ["lose heart" is used in the sense of cowardly surrender]. Even though our outward man is perishing, yet the inward man is being renewed day by day" (2 Corinthians 4:16). Paul puts the emphasis on what God has put within; he builds up his confidence in that. The perishing of the outward man is not always indicative of old age. Look at your own life; you have had the experience of sanctification and have been lifted into the heavenly places in Christ Jesus, and yet God's hand has been laid upon you. He has allowed the finger of decay to come to your body and lay you completely aside, and you begin to see what a slight hold you have on life, and the thought comes—"Well, I expect I will have to 'cave in.' I have not the strength I once had; I can never do the things I thought I would for God." This message is for you: "Though your outward man is perishing, yet your inward man is being renewed day by day."

The experience may not come with years but in the ordinary circumstances of life. It may come in a hundred and one ways and you realize that the outward man is wasting, that you have not the might you once had, and this is where the cowardly surrender is apt to come in—only we give it another name. The great craze today is to be healthy—"a sound mind in a sound body." Yet often the soundest minds have not been in sound bodies, but in very shaky tabernacles, and the word comes, "though our outward man is perishing, yet the inward man is being renewed day by day."

Paul faces the possibility of old age, decay, and death, with no rebellion and no sadness. Paul never hid from himself the effect that his work had upon him; he knew it was killing him. Like his Master, he was old before his time; but there was no whining and no retiring from the work. Paul was not a fool; he did not waste his energy ridiculously, neither did he ignore the fact that it was his genuine apostolic work and nothing else that was wearing him out. Michelangelo said a wonderful thing: "The more the marble wears, the better the image grows," and it is an illustration of this truth. Every wasting of nerve and brain in work for God brings a corresponding uplift and strengthening to spiritual muscle and fiber.

A good test for a worker is to ask this question: Does my inner life wing itself higher with every wearing of the body in work for God? If we are going to walk in the experimental knowledge of sanctification and live where God wants us to live, we must be willing to spend and be spent to the last ebb. But if the outward man is perishing because of an injudicious waste of physical strength or because of wrong habits, then it will always make us faint or "cave in." And if we give up prayer and communion with God, then the decay goes on to a terrible extent; there is no corresponding inward weight of glory, no inner winging.

The apostle Paul continually had external depression. He had agonies and distresses, terrible persecution and tumults in his life, but he never had the "blues," simply because he had learned the secret that the measure of the inner glory is the wasting of the outward man. The outer man was being wasted, Paul knew it and felt it, but the inner man was being renewed. Every wasting meant a corresponding winging on the inside. Some of us are so amazingly lazy, so comfortably placed in life, that we get no inner winging. The natural life, apart altogether from sin, must be sacrificed to the will and the word of God; otherwise there is no spiritual glory for the individual. With some of us the body is not wearing away. Our souls are stagnant, and the vision spiritually is not getting brighter. But once we get into the heavenlies, live there, and work from that standpoint, we find we have the glorious opportunity of spending all our bodily energies in God's service, and a corresponding weight of moral and spiritual glory remains all the time.

One of the most enervating things that can come across your life as a saint is the sympathy of others who do not understand the vision of your heart. They say, "Poor soul, you do suffer; so many people misunderstand you; you are put in such awkward circumstances." The thing to realize is that God enlarges us on the inside, not externally, and that every bit of nervous energy spent by us in

God's work means a grander weight of glory and spiritual insight. No matter how wearied or expended the body may be in God's work, there is the winging of the inner man into a higher grasp of God.

We have to beware of the pagan notion that our spirit develops in spite of our body. It develops *with* our body, and the way that spiritual insight develops in the worker is, as Paul states here, in the wasting of energy for God, because in this way the inner man is being renewed. It is not a question of saying, "Oh, my body is so lazy, I must drag it up to do something," but a question of working on God's line to the last lap, spending and being spent for one purpose only, and that purpose God's. If we put the body and the concerns of the body before the eternal weight of glory, we will never have any inner winging at all. We will always be asking God to patch up this old tabernacle and keep it in repair. But when the heart sees what God wants, and knows that the body must be willing to spend and be spent for that cause and that cause alone, then the inner man gets wings.

## The Beautifying Work

Balancing the ways. The apostle Paul soars above the things that are wearing out his physical life, not by sublime indifference, but by realizing the weight of glory which these very afflictions are working in him. Have you got hold of this secret that if you are right with God, the very thing that is an affliction to you is working out an eternal weight of glory? The afflictions may come from good people or from bad people, but behind the whole thing is God. Whenever Paul tries to state the unfathomable joy and glory that he has in the heavenlies in Christ Jesus, it is as if he cannot find words to express his meaning. In order to try to express it here he balances his words. For instance, "affliction" is matched with "glory"; "light"

is matched with "weight"; and "moment" is matched with "eternal."
I wonder if we balance our words like that?

In Romans 8:18, "For I consider that the sufferings of this present time are not worthy to be compared with the glory which shall be revealed in us," Paul is stating that it is the standpoint of the worker that determines everything. If you think of suffering affliction you will begin to write your own epitaph, begin to dream of the kind of tombstone you would like. That is the wrong standpoint. Have your standpoint in the heavenlies, and you will not think of the afflictions but only of the marvelous way God is working out the inner weight of glory all the time. You will hail with delight the afflictions that our Lord tells us to expect (John 16:33), the afflictions of which James writes (James 1:2), and of which Peter writes (1 Peter 4:12). Our Lord presented truth in "nugget" form, and in the epistles the apostles beat out these "nuggets" into negotiable gold.

"For our light affliction, which is but for a moment, is working for us a far more exceeding and eternal weight of glory" (2 Corinthians 4:17)). The apostle Paul seems to be putting things the wrong way round. Surely the affliction is the heavy thing and the glory the light thing! No, Paul is putting it in the right way; he puts the emphasis on the weight of glory resulting from the light affliction. Again, everything is determined by the standpoint you take. Stand in the heavenly places in Christ Jesus, and when the afflictions come you will praise the Lord, not with a sickly smile but with every bit of you, because you have learned the secret of the eternal weight of glory, and you know that His yoke is easy.

"For our light affliction, which is but for a moment. . . ." Paul seems to say, "Even if it were all tribulation, it would not matter, because the glory beginning already and the glory to come would make amends for it all." This law of glory working out of decay is God's beautifying work in a saint. The soother of all affliction is the steadfast thought of the glory that is being worked out by the afflictions. Paul here beats out the nugget of truth in our Lord's rebuke to Peter: "'Far be it from You, Lord; this shall not happen to You!' But He turned and said to Peter, 'Get behind Me, Satan'" (Matthew 16:22–23). Self-pity is taking the wrong standpoint, and if self-pity is indulged in, before long we will take part in the decaying thing instead of in that which grows more and more into the glory of God's presence.

## The Blessed Vision

**The watchword of other-worldliness.** The sanctified saint has to alter the horizon of other people's lives, and he does it by showing that they can be lifted onto a higher plane by the grace of God, namely, into the heavenly places in Christ Jesus. If you look at the horizon from the seashore, you will not see much of the sea; but climb higher up the cliff, and as you rise higher the horizon keeps level with your eye and you see more in between. Paul is seated in the heavenly places, and he can see the whole world mapped out in God's plan. He is looking ahead like a watchman, and his words convey the calm, triumphant contemplation of a conqueror. Some of us get distracted because we have not this world-wide outlook, we see only the little bit inside our own "bandbox." The apostle Paul has burst his bandbox. He has been lifted up onto a new plane in Christ Jesus and he sees now from His standpoint.

The preacher and the worker must learn to look at life as a whole. When we are lifted up to where Jesus is, it is not as if we were standing on a high pinnacle like a spiritual acrobat, balancing on one leg for two seconds and then tumbling. God lifts us up to a totally new plane, where there is plenty of room to live and to grow and to understand things from His standpoint. We see life as a whole. We see not only the glory that now is, but the glory that is yet to be.

"While we do not look at the things which are seen, but at the things which are not seen" (2 Corinthians 4:18). The "things not seen" refers not only to the glorious reward and the life yet to be, but to the invisible things in our present life on which our Lord's teaching centers, and on which the afflictions center. So many of us think only of the visible things, whereas the real concentration, the whole dead-set of the life, should be where our Lord put it in the huge nugget of truth, which we call the Sermon on the Mount. There our Lord says, in effect, "Take no thought for your life. Be carefully careless about everything saving one thing, your relationship to God." Naturally, we are apt to be carefully careless about everything saving that one thing.

The afflictions tackle these unseen centers of our life and we have to face them in the power of the indwelling Spirit of God. And if we have been lifted up into the heavenlies, we shall find that the battlings are bringing out more and more the eternal weight of glory, while we look at the things that are not seen. Do not think only of what is yet to be; think of the invisible things that are here and now. Think of the weight of glory that may be yours by means of that difficult person you have to live with, by means of the circumstances you are in, the people you come in contact with day by day. The phrase "a means of grace" comes with a wonderfully new meaning when we think of it in this light.

These words of the apostle Paul bring to us a message of invincible consolation. If you are a child of God and there is some part of your circumstances that is tearing you, if you are living in the heavenly places you will thank God for the tearing thing. If you are not in the heavenly places, you cry to God over and over again, "O Lord, remove this thing from me. If only I could live in golden streets and be surrounded with angels, and have the Spirit of God consciously indwelling me all the time and have everything wonderfully sweet, then I think I might be a Christian." That is not being a Christian. A Christian is one who can live in the midst of the trouble and turmoil with the glory of God indwelling him, while he steadfastly looks not at the things that are seen, but at the things that are not seen.

We have to learn to think of things that are seen only as a glorious chance of enabling us to concentrate on the things that are not seen. God engineers external things to reveal to us whether we are living in this imperturbable place of unutterable strength and glory, namely, the life hid with Christ in God. If we are, then let the troubles and difficulties work as they may on the outside, for we are confident that they are working out a grander weight of glory in the heavenlies.

## Things as They Are

We then, *as* workers together *with Him* also plead with *you* not to receive the grace of God in vain. For He says:

" In an acceptable time I have heard you,
And in the day of salvation I have helped you."

Behold, now *is* the accepted time; behold, now *is* the day of salvation.

We give no offense in anything, that our ministry may not be blamed. But in all *things* we commend ourselves as ministers of God: in much patience, in tribulations, in needs, in distresses, in stripes, in imprisonments, in tumults, in labors, in sleeplessness, in fastings; by purity, by knowledge, by longsuffering, by kindness, by the Holy Spirit, by sincere love, by the word of truth, by the power of God, by the armor of righteousness on the right hand and on the left, by honor and dishonor, by evil report and good report; as deceivers, and *yet* true; as unknown, and *yet* well known; as dying, and behold we live; as chastened, and *yet* not killed; as sorrowful, yet always rejoicing; as poor, yet making many rich; as having nothing, and *yet* possessing all things. (2 Corinthians 6:1–10)

We have to remain true to God in the midst of things as they are, to allow things as they are to transmute us. "Things as they are" are the very means God uses to make us into the praise of His glory. We have to live on this sordid earth, amongst human beings who are exactly like ourselves, remembering that it is on this plane that we have to work out the marvelous life God has put in us. Holiness in a human being is only manifested by means of antagonism. Physically, we are healthy according to our power of fight on the inside; morally, we are virtuous according to our moral caliber—virtue is always acquired; and spiritually, if we are drawing on the resurrection life of Jesus, spiritual stamina comes as we learn to "score off" the things that come against us, and in this way we produce a holy character.

The life of a worker is not a hop, skip and a jump affair; it is a squaring of the shoulders, then a steady, steadfast tramp straight through until we get to understand God's way. It takes the energy of God Himself to prepare a worker for all He wants to make him. We need a spiritual vision of work as well as a spiritual vision of truth. It is not that we go through a certain curriculum and then we are fit to work; preparation and work are so involved that they cannot be separated. The apostle Paul always comes right down to the practical. One of the outstanding miracles of God's grace is to make us able to take any kind of leadership at all without losing spiritual power. There is no more searching test in the whole of Christian life than that.

## The Worth to God

"We then, as workers together with Him" (2 Corinthians 6:1). When a worker has led a soul to Christ, his work has only just begun. Our attitude is apt to be—so many saved, so many sanctified, and then we shout "Hallelujah." But it is only then that the true work of the worker begins. It is then that we have to be held in God's hand and let the word of God be driven through us. It is then that we have to be put under the millstone and ground, put into the kneading trough and mixed properly, and then baked—all in order to be made broken bread to feed God's children.

"Go therefore, and make disciples" (Matthew 28:19). How many disciples have you made? Have you made one? Discipling is our work. When God's great redemptive work has issued in lives in salvation and sanctification, then the work of the worker begins. It is then that we find the meaning of being "workers together with Him," and the meaning of the apostle Paul's agony of heart and mind over his converts: "My little children, for whom I labor in birth again until Christ is formed in you" (Galatians 4:19). He waited, watched, longed, prayed, and worked until he could see them rooted and grounded in God.

Look at the laborious way of a scientist in finding out the secrets of nature, and then look at our own slipshod ignorance with regard to God's Book. If the worker will obey God's way, he will find he has to be everlastingly delving into the Bible and working it out in circumstances; the two always run together. It requires all the machinery of circumstances to bring a worker where God wants him to be—"workers together with Him."

We are apt to say, "Now I am fitted for this particular work because of my natural temperament, and I intend to work only along this line." An exclusive worker is excluded by God, because God does not work in that way. The gifts of the Spirit are distributed "to each one individually as He wills" (1 Corinthians 12:11); they are entirely of God and they all work together with God. The worth of a worker to God is just the worth of a man's own fingers to his brain.

## The Wooing of God

"We . . . plead with you not to receive the grace of God in vain" (2 Corinthians 6:1). The wooing of God is not the same as the wooing of man. The wooing of a man's personality may often hinder the wooing of God. The apostle Paul's pleading is caught up into the entreaty of the Spirit of God so that it is the wooing of God that is working through him, "as though God were pleading through us" (2 Corinthians 5:20). This is the entreaty that is learned at Calvary and made real in the worker by the Holy Spirit.

It is not the tones of a man's speech, or the passion of a man's personality; it is the pleading power of the Holy Spirit coming through him. Consequently the worker has no sympathy with things with which God's Spirit has no sympathy. We are in danger of being stern where God is tender, and of being tender where God is stern. The apostle Paul so identifies his own beseeching and passion with the entreaty of God that the two are identical. He is afraid "lest somehow . . . your minds may be corrupted from the simplicity that is in Christ" (2 Corinthians 11:3).

## The World's Coarse Thumb

"We give no offense in anything" (2 Corinthians 6:3). The worldling is annoyed at the worker because the worker is always dealing with a crisis that he does not see and does not want to see. No matter what he touches on, the worker always comes back to the claim of God, and the worldling gets annoyed at this. The man of the world analyzes the easy parts of life and tells you that these are all quite obvious, that all the practical outcomes of life are within his reach. But when the worker begins to touch on God's message, he says, "That is nonsense. You are up in the clouds and unpractical." That is why the worker's voice is always an annoyance to the worldling.

"That our ministry may not be blamed" (2 Corinthians 6:3). The world is glad of an excuse not to listen to the gospel message, and the inconsistencies of Christians is made the excuse. "Woe to the world because of offenses!" said our Lord. "For offenses come, but woe to that man by whom the offense comes!" (Matthew 18:7). Offense means something to strike up against, and the world is on the watch for that kind of thing. If a worker is tripped in private life, the world strikes against that at once and makes it the excuse for not accepting the gospel. The perilous possibility of being an occasion of stumbling is always there. Paul never forgot the possibility of it in his own life, "lest when I have preached to others, I myself should become disqualified" (1 Corinthians 9:27). The only safeguard is living the life hid with Christ in God, and a steady watchfulness that we walk in the light as God is in the light.

## The Wheel of Circumstances

"But in all things we commend ourselves as ministers of God: in much patience, in tribulations, in needs, in distresses, in stripes, in imprisonments, in tumults, in labors, in sleeplessness, in fastings" (2 Corinthians 6: 4–5) Read the life of the apostle Paul and you find that he drank to the last dregs the experience of every one of the things mentioned in these verses. Paul is not indulging in oratory; he is stating the things God put him through. All his experiences called for patience. Holiness can only be worked out in and through the din of things as they are. God does not slide holiness into our hearts like a treasure box from heaven—we open the lid and out it comes. Holiness works out in us as it worked out in our Lord. The holiness of God Almighty is absolute; that is, it knows no development by antagonism. The holiness exhibited by the Son of God, and by God's children, is the holiness that expresses itself by means of antagonism.

There are some wonderful words in verses 4 and 5: "In much *patience*"—patience is the result of well-centered strength; it takes the strength of almighty God to keep a man patient. No one can remain under and endure what God puts a servant of His through unless he has the power of God. We read that our Lord was "crucified through weakness," yet it took omnipotent might to make Him weak like that. Where is the impulsive enthusiasm that is manifested at the start of the Christian life? Has it all gone? No, it has been transmuted into the strength that can be weak. "*In tribulations*"—tribulation or affliction (KJV) is something that crushes like a weight until you have not a word to say. "*In needs*"—the loss of liberty, confinement. A happy heart and an unpaid salary, a high head and an empty pocket—that is the way it works out in reality. "*In distresses*"—perplexities such as sickness, the loss of friends, the inscrutable ways of God's providence, but through it all the grace of God comes, it is an inner unconquerableness. "*In stripes, in imprisonments, in tumults, in labors, in sleeplessness, in fastings*"—in all these things manifest the drawing on the grace of God that makes you a marvel to yourself and to others. Draw now, not presently. The one word in the spiritual vocabulary is *now*. Let circumstances bring you where they will, and keep drawing on the grace of God. One of the greatest proofs that you are drawing on the grace of God is that you can be humiliated without manifesting the slightest trace of anything but His grace in you.

Verses 4–10 are Paul's spiritual diary. They describe the outward hardships that proved the hotbed for the graces of the Spirit—the working together of outward hardships and inward grace. You have been asking the Lord to give you the graces of the Spirit, and then some set of circumstances has come and given you a sharp twinge, and you say, "Well, I have asked God to bring out in me the graces of the Spirit, but every time the devil seems to get the better of me." What you are calling "the devil" is the very thing God is using to manifest the graces of the Spirit in you.

"By honor and dishonor, by evil report and good report." The worker learns the secret of the "campfires" where he can recount with other Christians the great hours when the Son of God walked with him in the fiery furnace. The thing that keeps us off enchanted ground is to remember that we are on God's campaigns, that we have no certain place of abode, no nesting place here.

> He fixed thee midst this dance
> Of plastic circumstance,
> This Present, thou, forsooth, would'st fain arrest:
> Machinery just meant
> To give thy soul its bent,
> Try thee and turn thee forth, sufficiently impressed.

The fiery furnaces are there by God's direct permission. It is misleading to imagine that we are developed in spite of our circumstances. We are developed because of them. It is mastery *in* circumstances that is needed, not mastery over them. We have to manifest the graces of the Spirit amongst things as they are, not to wait for the millennium.

## The Wine of God

In 2 Corinthians 6:7–10 the apostle Paul is giving out golden truths from his own experience. Paul's external life had been spilt and rent, and crushed and broken; then out of it came the wine of God. Wine comes only from crushed grapes, and the things Paul mentions here are the things that bring out the wine that God likes.

You cannot be poured-out wine if you remain a whole grape; you cannot be broken bread if you remain whole grain. Grapes have to be crushed, and grain has to be ground; then the sweetness of the life comes out to the glory of God. Watch the circumstances of life. We get them fairly well mixed, and if we are getting more than enough of one kind, let us thank the Lord for it. It is producing the particular grace that God wants us to manifest.

# THE
# MAKING
## OF A
# CHRISTIAN

# CHAPTER ONE

*The ascendancy which He exercised in thus drawing men away from worldly callings and hopes into association with Himself is quite indefinite, and even in yielding to it, the disciples could have no distinct idea what it involved.*

—Dr. James Denney

## Days of His Flesh

### The Dominating Sentiment (Matthew 4:18–22; Mark 1:16–20; John 1:35–42)

The average preaching of redemption deals mainly with the "scenic" cases; that is, those who have gone through exceptional experiences. But none of the early disciples had these scenic experiences, nor was their dominating sentiment a desire for deliverance from sin. They were elemental men in touch with the forces of nature, and there was something about Jesus Christ that fascinated them. When He said, "Follow Me," they followed Him at once; it was no cross to them. It would have been a cross not to follow, for the spell of Jesus was on them.

We have come to the conclusion nowadays that a man must be a conscious sinner before Jesus Christ can do anything for him. The early disciples were not attracted to Jesus because they wanted to be saved from sin; they had no concept that they needed saving. They were attracted to Him by a dominating sincerity, by sentiments other than those that we say make men come to Jesus. There was nothing theological in their following, no consciousness of passing from death unto life, no knowledge of what Jesus meant when He talked about His cross. It was on the plane where all was natural, although mysterious and wonderful.

The call of God comes only to the affinity of God in a person, and is always implicit. The beginnings of moral ascension in a person's life are never definite, but always deep down in the depths of his personality where he cannot trace. These early disciples were not trammeled by possessions, and when the dominating sentiment of sincerity in their own lives was met by the fascination of Jesus, they yielded at once. They did not follow Jesus because they wanted to be saved, but because they could not help following. Three years later when again Jesus said, "Follow Me," it was a different matter. Many things had happened during those years. The first "Follow Me" meant an external following. Now it was to be a following in internal martyrdom (see John 21:18–19).

# Days of Our Flesh

## The Dominating Sincerity (1 Peter 2:21)

The attitude of the early disciples was one of self-ignorance. Jesus Christ knew perfectly well what was in them, but He did not say to John, "You will prove to be vindictive" (see Luke 9:51–55), or to Peter, "You will end in denying Me" (see Mark 14:66–72). If you had told Peter that he would deny Jesus with oaths and curses, he would have been amazed (see John 13:36–38). Jesus Christ taught the disciples the truth, and left them with the atmosphere of His own life, and slowly they began to see things differently. The disciples approached Jesus by the way of sincerity, and He put them through crises until they discovered that they could never be disciples in that way; what they needed was to have the disposition of Jesus given to them. The disciples were fascinated by Jesus. When He said, "Follow Me," they immediately left all and followed Him, and yet after three years of the closest intimacy, "they all forsook Him and fled" (Mark 14:50). Their following ended in disaster.

The majority of men are attracted to Jesus on the same line as the early disciples were. The disciples were brought to a knowledge of themselves, and we have to come to a knowledge of ourselves in the same way. We have to realize that human sincerity will never stand the strain when the ideals that fascinate a man's mind come in contact with actual life. The disaster may not be external, but in his heart a man says: "I honestly tried my best to serve Jesus Christ. I did decide for Him. In all sincerity I gave all I had to the ideals He presents, but I cannot go on. The New Testament presents ideals beyond my attainment. I won't lower my ideals, although I can never hope to make them actual." Our Lord says to such a one, "Come to Me . . . and I will give you rest" (Matthew 11:28), or "I will make the ideal actual." But a sense of need must arise first. As long as we deal with abstractions, we have no sense of need.

Apart from Jesus Christ there is an unbridgeable gap between the ideal and the actual; the only way out is a personal relationship to Him. The early disciples were put through crises in order to reveal them to themselves. Jesus was never in a hurry with them; He never explained; He simply stated the truth and told them that when the Holy Spirit was come, "He will teach you all things and bring to your remembrance all things that I said to you" (John 14:26).

Today Jesus Christ is at work in ways we cannot tabulate. Lives are being drawn to Him in a thousand and one incalculable ways. An atmosphere is being created, seeds are being sown, and men are being drawn nearer to the point where they will see Him.

# Chapter Two

They could do what they could not do before, because He enabled them to do it, and the sense of this is a rudimentary form of this specifically Christian consciousness. –Dr. James Denney

## Days of His Flesh

The dominating sentiment that attracted the early disciples to Jesus was not a sense of conviction of sin; they had no violent sin to turn from, and consequently no conscious need of salvation. They were not sinners in the ordinary accepted sense of the term, but honest, sincere men, and they were attracted to Jesus by something more difficult to state than the desire for deliverance from sin. The spell of Jesus was on them, and when He said, "Follow Me," they followed at once, although they could have had no idea what the following would involve. The call of God is never articulate; it is always implicit.

There was in the disciples the "one fact more," which put them in one kingdom and Jesus Christ in another kingdom. Our Lord was never impatient. He simply planted seed thoughts in their minds and surrounded them with the atmosphere of His own life. He did not attempt to convince them, but left mistakes to correct themselves, because He knew that eventually the truth would bear fruit in their lives.

How differently we would have acted. We get impatient and take men by the scruff of the neck and say, "You must believe this and that." You cannot make a man see moral truth by persuading his intellect. "When He, the Spirit of truth, has come, He will guide you into all truth" (John 16:13).

## The Desire to Serve (Matthew 20:22)

"Jesus answered and said, . . . 'Are you able to drink the cup that I am about to drink?' . . .They say to Him, 'We are able'" (Matthew 20:22). The disciples would have gone to any length to prove their devotion to Jesus (see Matthew 26:35). It was true devotion, but it wilted because it was based on an entire ignorance of themselves. In the end they "all forsook Him and fled," not because they wanted to, but because they did not know how to go on. Jesus put the disciples through crises to reveal them to themselves and bring them to the place of receiving the Holy Spirit. They could not see their need to receive the Holy Spirit until they found out that they were spiritual paupers. "Simon, Simon! Indeed, Satan has asked for you, that he may sift you as wheat" (Luke 22:31). Jesus allowed Peter to go over a moral precipice and deny that he ever knew Him so that Peter would realize what it was that kept him from being a disciple. It is not necessary for everyone to go the way of Peter's sifting, but the sifting must come in some form or other. The preaching of the gospel of temperament will not do for the making of disciples, nor will Jesus shield us in the slightest degree from any of the requirements of discipleship.

The early disciples were honest, sincere, zealous men. They had given up everything to follow Jesus; their sense of the heroic was grand. But where did it all end? "They all forsook Him and fled." They came to realize that no human earnestness or sincerity on earth can ever begin to fulfil what Jesus demands of a disciple.

Then after the resurrection, Jesus "breathed on them, and said to them, 'Receive the Holy Spirit'" (John 20:22). They had come to the end of themselves and all self-sufficiency, and in their destitution they were willing to receive the gift of the Holy Spirit. "Their eyes were opened and they knew Him" (Luke 24:31). Their inner consciousness was opened; there was a totally new power on the inside. They could do what they could not do before, because He enabled them to do it. But they had first of all to be brought within the moral frontier of need before they realized they were powerless to live and move in the kingdom where Jesus lived.

# Days of Our Flesh

## The Determination to Serve (Luke 10:20)

Natural devotion may be all very well to attract men and women to Jesus, to make them feel the fascination of His claims; but natural devotion will never make a disciple. It will always deny Jesus somewhere or other. Today, as in the days of His flesh, men and women are being drawn to Jesus by their dominating sincerity, but human sincerity is not enough to make a person a disciple of Jesus Christ. There are many today who are sincere, but they are not real; they are not hypocrites, but perfectly honest and earnest and desirous of fulfilling what Jesus wants of them, but they *really* cannot do it because they have not received the Holy Spirit who will make them real.

The phrase we hear so often, "Decide for Christ," is most misleading, because it puts the emphasis on the wrong thing, and is apt to present Jesus Christ in a false way as Someone in need of our allegiance. A decision cannot hold forever, because a person is the same after making it as before, and there will be a reaction sooner or later. Whenever a man or woman fails in personal experience, it is because he or she has never *received* anything. There is always a positive difference when something has been received—new powers begin to manifest themselves. Nothing has any power to alter a person save the incoming of the life of Jesus, and that is the only sign that the person is born again.

The bedrock in Jesus Christ's kingdom is not sincerity, not deciding for Christ, not a determination to serve Him, but a complete and entire recognition that we cannot begin to do it. Then, says Jesus, "Blessed are you." Jesus Christ can do wonderful things for the person who enters into His kingdom through the moral frontier of need. Decisions for Christ fail not because men are not in earnest, but because the bedrock of Christianity is ignored. The bedrock of Christianity does not lie in vowing or in strength of will. To begin with, it is not ethical at all, but simply the recognition of the fact that I have not the power within me to do what my spirit longs to do. "Come unto Me," said Jesus, not "Decide for Me." When I realize my inability to be what the New Testament tells me I should be, I have to come to Jesus "just as I am." I realize that I am an abject pauper, morally and spiritually; if ever I am going to be what Jesus wants me to be, He must come in and do it. Jesus Christ claims, on the basis of His redemption, that He can put His own disposition into anyone who is consciously poor enough to receive it; that is, the ability not only to will but to do (see Philippians 2:12–13). The knowledge of our own poverty brings us to the moral frontier where Jesus Christ works.

If you are trying to live up to a standard of belief and find you have not the power to do it, be humble enough to recognize that Jesus Christ knows more about the matter than you do. He has pledged His Father's honor to give you the Holy Spirit if you ask Him: "If you then, being evil, know how to give good gifts to your children, how much more will your heavenly Father give the Holy Spirit to those who ask Him?" (Luke 11:13). The Holy Spirit at work in our personal lives enables us to make the ideal and the actual one, and we begin slowly to discern that we have been brought into the place where Jesus Christ tells. The beginning of spiritual life is deep down where it cannot be traced; the theological explanation will emerge presently. The first thing a man or woman needs is to be born into the kingdom of God by receiving the Holy Spirit, and then slowly and surely be turned into a disciple. The entrance into the kingdom of God is always through the moral frontier of need. At any turn of the road the touch may come.

# CHAPTER THREE

The Holy Spirit is the missing factor in our personality,
and without it we cannot be altogether as God wants us to
be. An abiding gift makes an abiding change in the person
to whom the gift is made. —Selby

## In the Days of His Resurrection

Jesus put the early disciples through crises until they discovered
that they could not be disciples by means of ordinary human sincerity and devotion. Human earnestness and vowing cannot make a
person a disciple of Jesus Christ any more than it can turn him into
an angel; something must be received by each person, and that is the
meaning of being born again. When one is struck by his need of the
Holy Spirit, God will put the Holy Spirit into his spirit. In regeneration, the personal spirit is energized by the Holy Spirit, and the
Son of God is formed in him (see Galatians 1:15–16; 4:19). This is
the New Testament evangel, and it needs to be restated. New birth
refers not only to a person's eternal salvation, but to his being of
value to God in this order of things; it means infinitely more than
being delivered from sin and from hell. The gift of the essential nature of God is made efficacious in us by the entering in of the Holy
Spirit; He imparts to us the quickening life of the Son of God, and
we are lifted into the domain where Jesus lives (see John 3:5).

Our creeds teach us to believe in the Holy Spirit, and the New Testament says we must receive Him. The person who is crumpled up with sin is the one who most quickly comes to realize his need. It takes the upright man a long while to realize that his natural virtues are the remnants of a design that has been broken, and that the only way the design can be fulfilled is by his being made all over again. "Do not marvel that I said to you, 'You must be born again'" (John 3:7). The bedrock in Jesus Christ's kingdom is poverty, not possession; weakness, not strength of will; infirmity of character, not goodness; a sense of absolute poverty, not decisions for Christ. "Blessed are the poor in spirit" (Matthew 5:3). That is the entrance, and it takes a long time to bring us to a knowledge of our own poverty. The greatest blessing we ever get from God is to know that we are destitute spiritually.

## The Revelation of Christ (Luke 24:16, 31)

The disciples were with Jesus for three years, but they only once discerned Him—in the one intuitive flash recorded in Matthew 16, when it was revealed to Peter who Jesus was. Our Lord never sent the disciples out on the ground that He had done something for them, but only on the ground that they had seen Him (see John 9:35–38; 10:14–18). Mary Magdalene had had seven devils cast out of her, but it was not until Jesus revealed Himself to her after His resurrection that He said, "Go and tell My brethren" (Matthew 28:10). The man who has seen Jesus can never be daunted; the man who has only a personal testimony as to what Jesus has done for him may be daunted, but nothing can turn the man who has seen Him; he endures "as seeing Him who is invisible" (Hebrews 11:27).

Is my knowledge of Jesus born of inner spiritual perception, or is it only what I have learned by listening to others? Have I something in my life that connects me with the Lord Jesus as my personal

Savior? All spiritual history must have a personal knowledge for its bedrock.

## In the Days of Our Regeneration

Every person has need of new birth. "Most assuredly, I say to you, unless one is born again, he cannot see the kingdom of God" (John 3:3). Jesus did not speak these words to a man down and out in sin, but to a sterling, worthy, upright man. The concept of new birth in the New Testament is not a concept of something that springs out of us, but of something that enters into us. Just as our Lord came into human history from without, so He must come into us from without. Our new birth is the birth of the life of the Son of God into our old human nature, and our human nature has to be transfigured by the indwelling life of the Son of God.

Have I allowed my personal human life to become a "Bethlehem" for the Son of God? It is not that God patches up my natural virtues, but that I learn by obedience to make room for Jesus Christ to exhibit His disposition in me. It is impossible to imitate the disposition of Jesus. Am I becoming the birthplace of the Son of God (see Luke 1:35), or do I only know the miracle of God's changing grace?

### The Realization of Christ (John 20:28)

The one great characteristic of being born from above is that I know who Jesus is. It is a discernment: something has happened on the inside; the surgery of events has opened my eyes. Is Jesus Christ a revelation to me, or is He simply an historical character? How are we to get the revelation of who Jesus is? Very simply. Jesus said that the Holy Spirit would glorify Him, and we can receive the Holy Spirit by asking (see Luke 11:13). Then we too shall be in the same category with Peter, and Jesus will say, "Blessed are you . . . for flesh and blood has not revealed this to you, but My Father who is in heaven" (Matthew 16:17). We can only know the Father through the Son (see Matthew 11:27), and regeneration means that God puts into my spirit the Spirit of His Son. Ask God on the authority of Jesus to give you the Holy Spirit, and He will do so; but you will never ask until you have struck the bottom board of your need.

When I asked God to give me the Holy Spirit, He did so, and what a transformation took place! Life became heaven on earth after being hell on earth. Never say that Jesus has done in you what you know He has not done. God comes to you the instant He is asked, and you will realize the difference in actual experience. When things happen you are amazed at the change that has been wrought, not by an effort of your will, but by banking on the new power within.

When we receive the Holy Spirit, we receive the quickening life that lifts us into the domain where Jesus lives, and we have the revelation of who He is. The secret of the Christian is that he knows the absolute deity of Jesus Christ. Has Jesus made any difference to us in our actual life? The essence of Christianity is not a creed or a doctrine, but an illumination that emancipates us—"I see who Jesus is." It is always a surprise, never an intellectual concept. "The wind blows where it wishes . . . So *is everyone who is born of the Spirit*" (John 3:8, emphasis added).

# CHAPTER FOUR

It is the true nature of the Pentecostal experience to produce a congruity between the message and the messenger.
The Gospel has to be proclaimed, it has to be commended,
it has to be announced, but it has to be adorned. The Holy
Ghost will fall on those who hear the word when it has
fallen on those who speak the word. —Selby

My spiritual life is based on some word of God made living in me;
when I transact on that word, I step into the moral frontier where
Jesus works. He says, "Come unto Me" . . . "Ask, and it shall be
given you." Commitment is always required. An intellectual never
pushes an issue of will. Our Lord uses the word "believe" in a moral
sense, not in an intellectual sense. "Commit yourself to Me." We
are to believe in a person, not to believe for something. "This is
the work of God, that you believe in Him whom He sent" (John
6:29). Christianity is not a matter of deciding for Christ, nor of
making vows, but of receiving something from God on the basis
of His promise in Luke 11:13. The reception of the Holy Spirit
is the maintained attitude of the believer by "being filled with the
Spirit." The way of His entrance into us is the knowledge of our
own poverty.

# In the Days of His Resurrection

## The Promise of the Highest (Acts 1:4; Luke 24:49–53)

The reason the disciples had to tarry until the day of Pentecost was not merely that they might be fitted to receive the promise. They had to wait until the Lord was glorified historically, for the Holy Spirit did not descend until the Son of God was glorified and ascended to the right hand of the Father (see John 15:26; Acts 2:33). The parenthesis in John 7:39—"for the Holy Spirit was not yet given, because Jesus was yet glorified"— does not apply to us. The Holy Spirit has been given; Jesus has been glorified. Now the waiting depends upon our fitness, not upon God's providence. The reception of the Holy Spirit depends entirely upon moral preparation. I must abide in the light that the Holy Spirit sheds and be obedient to the word of God. Then when the power of God comes upon such obedience there will be the manifestation of a strong family likeness to Jesus. It is easier to be swayed by emotions than to live a life shot through with the Holy Spirit, a life in which Jesus is glorified. The Holy Spirit is absolutely honest; He indicates the things that are right and the things that are wrong.

"Tarry . . . until . . . " (Luke 24:49). This is the New Testament concept of fasting, not from food only but from everything, until the particular thing we have been told to expect is fulfilled. Fasting means concentration in order that the purpose of God may be developed in our lives.

"Until you are endued with power from on high" (Luke 24:49). There is only one "power from on high"—a holy power that transfigures morality. Never yield to a power unless you know its character. Spiritualism is more than trickery; it has hold of powers that are not characterized by the holy integrity of Jesus.

Jesus Christ gives the power of His own disposition to carry us through, if we are willing to obey. That is why He is apparently so merciless to those of us who have received the Holy Spirit, because He makes His demands according to *His* disposition, not according to our natural disposition. On the basis of the redemption, God expects us to erect characters worthy of the sons of God. He does not expect us to carry on "evangelical capers," but to manifest the life of the Son of God in our mortal flesh.

# In the Days of Our Regeneration

### The Sovereign Preference (John 21:15–17)

Our Lord here is not only reinstating Peter, but laying down the basis of the apostolic office, and He bases it on love. "Do you love Me more than these?" There is not the slightest strand of delusion left in Peter's mind about himself; he has come to an end of all his self-sufficiency (see John 13:37), and the question of his Lord is a revelation to him as to how much he does love Him—"Lord, You know all things; You know that I love You." Love is the sovereign preference of one person for another person, and when the Holy Spirit is in a man, that other Person is Jesus. The only lover of the Lord Jesus Christ is the Holy Spirit (see Romans 5:5). When a man has entered into a personal relationship with Jesus by means of the reception of the Holy Spirit, the first characteristic of that relationship is the nourishing of those who believe in Jesus. "Do you love Me? . . . Feed My sheep." That is what we are saved for, not to feed our converts, or to promulgate our explanation of things, but to be sent out by Christ, possessed of His Spirit, to feed His sheep. There is no release from that commission.

When we are young in grace, we go where we want to go. But Jesus says, "When you are old . . . another will gird you and carry you where you do not wish to go." This reference to Peter's death by crucifixion has a symbolic meaning for the real innerness of being fastened for discipline. It is this stage of spiritual experience that brings us into touch with the spirit of Jesus in that "even Christ did not please Himself" (Romans 15:3). This is the crisis of discipleship. We do not object to being delivered from sin, but we do not intend to give up the right to ourselves; it is this point that is balked. Jesus will never make us give up our right to ourselves; we must do it of our own deliberate choice. Our Lord always talks about discipleship with an "if." "If any man will be My disciple"—those are the conditions (see Luke 14:26–27, 33).

"And when He had spoken this, He said to him, 'Follow Me.'" When three years before Jesus said, "Follow Me," Peter did it easily; the fascination of Jesus was upon him, and he followed without any hesitation. But Peter did not know himself, and he came to the place where he denied Jesus with oaths and curses, and his heart broke. Then he received the Holy Spirit; and again Jesus says, "Follow Me." There is only one lodestar in Peter's life now—the Lord Jesus Christ. He is to follow Jesus now in the submission of his will and his intelligence to Him.

The way Jesus dealt with the disciples is the way He deals with us. He surrounded the disciples with an atmosphere of His own life and put in seed thoughts; that is, He stated His truth and left it to come to fruition. "I still have many things to say to you, but you cannot bear them now" (John 16:12); that is, you are not in the domain where you can understand. The disciples did not understand what Jesus taught them in the days of His flesh, but His teaching took on new meaning once they received the Holy Spirit (see John 14:26; 16:13).

Redemption means that Jesus Christ can give me His own disposition, and all the standards He gives are based on that disposition. *Jesus Christ's teaching is for the life He puts in.*

# CHAPTER FIVE

The victory that overcomes the world is not human love,
but Christian faith; it is not won by the natural heart, but
by the re-creating cross. –Peter Taylor Forsyth

## In the Days of His Ascension

### The Promise of Authoritative Lordship (Acts 1:8)

There is only one Lord of men, the Lord Jesus Christ, and yet
He never insists upon His authority; He never says "You shall."
He takes the patient course with us, as He did with the early disciples. When they received the Holy Spirit, He took absolute con-
trol of them, and Jesus Christ's teachings took on new meaning.
Naturally we do not pay any attention to what Jesus says unless
it is in agreement with our own conceptions; we come to realize
that Jesus Christ does not tell outside certain moral frontiers. The
teaching of Jesus only begins to apply to us when we have received
the disposition that ruled Him. Jesus Christ makes human des-
tiny depend entirely upon a man's relationship to Him (see John
3:36). According to our Lord, the bedrock of membership in the
Christian church is a personal revelation from God as to who Jesus
is, and a public declaration of it (see Matthew 15:15–19).

Our Lord taught His Lordship to His disciples and said that

after He had ascended He would send forth the Holy Spirit, who would be the disposer of affairs, both individual and international. We have not made Jesus Christ Lord; we have not given up the right to ourselves to Him; consequently we continually muddle our affairs by our own intuitions and desires for our own ends. Both nations and individuals have tried Christianity and abandoned it, because it has been found too difficult; but no man has ever gone through the crisis of deliberately making Jesus Lord and found Him to be a failure.

"God is no respecter of persons" (Acts 10:34 KJV). Christianity cuts out a man's personal prejudices. A moral earthquake was required before Peter recognized that God was the same to the crowd outside as to those within (see Acts 10). We are apt to imagine that God will only work according to precedent. The Holy Spirit is worldwide. God says that He will pour out His spirit "on all flesh" (Joel 2:28). Those who are not the servants of God may have a right vision in view for the human race, a vision of the time when men shall live as brothers. The difference does not lie in the vision, because the source of the vision is the Spirit of God; it lies in the way the vision is to be fulfilled. The servant of God knows that it can be fulfilled in only one way, namely, on the basis of redemption. "Your sons and your daughters" (Joel 2:28) refers to the men who have no concern about the redemptive point of view.

> The brotherhood of the New Testament is indeed meant to cover the race at last, but it is the brotherhood of Christian faith and love, not of mankind. —Peter Taylor Forsyth

All men are brothers, but they are not the brothers of Christ until they have become so by a moral likeness of disposition.

As our Lord ascended, He stretched forth His hands; the last the disciples saw of Jesus was His pierced hands. The pierced hands are emblematic of the atonement. "If anyone says to you, 'Look, here is the Christ!' or 'Look, He is there!' do not believe it" (Mark 13:21). The declaration of the angels was that it is "this same Jesus" who is to come again, with the marks of the atonement on Him. The wounded hands and feet are a symbol of the Redeemer who will come again. There are no marks of atonement in the "Labor Party Christ," or the "Socialist Christ," or the "Christian Science Christ."

# In the Days of Our Apprehension

## The Sacramental Personality (Ephesians 4:8–12)

Up to the time of the transfiguration, our Lord had exhibited the normal, perfect life of a man; after the transfiguration everything is unfamiliar to us. From the transfiguration onward, we are dealing not so much with the life our Lord lived as with the way in which He made it possible for us to enter into His life. On the Mount of Ascension the transfiguration was completed, and our Lord went back to His primal glory. But He did not go back simply as Son of God; He went back as Son of Man as well as Son of God. That means there is now freedom of access for anyone straight to the very throne of God through the ascension of the Son of Man. At His ascension our Lord entered Heaven, and He keeps the door open for humanity to enter.

Our Lord told the disciples that the sign of His ascension would be that He would send forth "the Promise of My Father" upon them (Luke 24:49). The Holy Spirit is not "this same Jesus"; He is the Bondservant of the Son of God, doing *in* human lives all that Jesus did *for* them. The Holy Spirit is in complete subjection to the person of the Redeemer for the purposes of redemption, as our Lord was in subjection to the Father (see John 5:19; 16:13).

Notice the gifts that the apostle Paul says Jesus sent after He ascended—apostles, prophets, evangelists, pastors and teachers—"for the equipping of the saints for the work of ministry, for the edifying of the body of Christ" (Ephesians 4:12). The test of a preacher or teacher is that as we listen to him we are built up in our faith in Jesus Christ and in our intimacy with Him; otherwise he is not a gift from God. Today we are apt to test the preacher on the ground of his personality and not by his building up of the saints.

"My sheep hear My voice," said Jesus (John 10:27)—preaching and teaching that comes from a central relationship to Himself. "Do you love Me? . . . Feed My sheep." Once the crisis of identification with Jesus is passed, the characteristic of the life is that we keep open house for the universe. The saint is at home anywhere on Mother Earth. He dare be no longer parochial or denominational; he belongs to no particular crowd, he belongs to Jesus Christ. A saint is a sacramental personality, one through whom the presence of God comes to others (see John 7:37–39).

"Till we all come to the unity of the faith . . . to the measure of the stature of the fullness of Christ" (Ephesians 4:13). The Holy Spirit builds us up into the body of Christ. All that Jesus Christ came to do is made ours experimentally by the Holy Spirit, and all His gifts are for the good of the whole body, not for individual exaltation. Individuality must go in order that the personal life may be brought out into fellowship with God. By the baptism of the Holy Spirit we are delivered from the husk of independent individuality; our personality is awakened and brought into communion with God.

We too often divorce what the New Testament never divorces. The baptism of the Holy Spirit is not an experience apart from Christ: it is the evidence of the ascended Christ. It is not the baptism of the Holy Spirit that changes men, but the power of the ascended Christ coming into men's lives by the Holy Spirit that changes them.

"You shall be witnesses to Me" (Acts 1:8). This great Pentecostal phrase puts the truth for us in unforgettable words. Witnesses not so much of what Jesus Christ can do, but *"witnesses to Me,"*—a delight to the heart of Jesus, a satisfaction to Him wherever He places us.

A saint's life is in the hands of God as a bow and arrow in the hands of an archer. God is aiming at something the saint cannot see; He stretches and strains, and every now and again the saint says, "I cannot stand any more." But God does not heed; He goes on stretching until His purpose is in sight, then He lets fly. We are here for God's designs, not for our own. We have to learn that this is the dispensation of the humiliation of the saints. The Christian church has blundered by not recognizing this. In another dispensation the manifestation of the saints will take place, but in this dispensation we are to be disciples of Jesus Christ, not following our own convictions but remaining true to Him.

The great lack today is of people who will *think* along Christian lines. We know a great deal about salvation, but we do not go on to explore the "unsearchable riches of Christ." We do not know much about giving up the right to ourselves to Jesus Christ, or about the intense patience of "hanging in," in perfect certainty that what Jesus says is true.

# NOW
## IS IT
# POSSIBLE—

# Now Is It Possible—

We never can be faultless in this life, but God's Book brings out that we must be blameless; that is, undeserving of censure from God's standpoint. And remember what His standpoint is. He can see into every crook and cranny of my spirit and soul and body, and He demands that I be blameless in all my relationships so that He Himself can see nothing worthy of censure. This revelation is one that shows the supernaturalness of the work of sanctification. It cannot be done by praying, by devoting myself, by believing; it can only be done by the supernatural power of a supernatural God.

## To Be Blameless in My Self-Life?

And may your whole spirit, soul, and body be preserved blameless at the coming of our Lord Jesus Christ. (1 Thessalonians 5:23)

Now where are we? Is there the tiniest element of the conviction of the Spirit of God? If so, yield to Him at once. We must distinguish between the working of our own suspicions and the checking of the Spirit of God who works as quietly and silently as a breeze. As He brings back to our mind our bodily life in this past week in public and in private, in eating and drinking, have we been blameless in our self-life? Sanctification means that God keeps my whole spirit and soul and body undeserving of censure in His sight.

Take the soul—how have we been conducting our imaginations, our motives, our fancies, and all the working of our reasoning life; is there anything for the Spirit of God to check and censure? We must not say because we are sanctified we are sure to be right. The seal of sanctification in the practical life is that it is blameless, undeserving of censure before God. Blamelessness is not faultlessness; faultlessness was the condition of the Lord Jesus Christ. We never can be faultless in this life; we are in impaired human bodies. But by sanctification we can be blameless. Our disposition can be supernaturally altered, until in the simplicity of life before God the whole limit is holy; and if that is to be done, it must be by the great grace of God. "My peace I give to you" (John 14:27). The Spirit of God works with an amazing zeal on Christ's words.

"May your whole spirit . . . be preserved blameless." Are we spiritually affected before God? Are our petitions our own? Do we put our will into them? Do we borrow our sentiments, or are they really ours? Paul does not say we are to be blameless in our self-life in the view of other people. We never shall be; Jesus Christ was not. It was said of His bodily life, "Look, a glutton and a winebibber"; of His soul life, "He . . . is mad"; and of His spirit life, "He has a demon" (Matthew 11:19; John 10:20). But before God He was blameless. Some of us are so concerned about being blameless before men that we are to be blamed before God. The apostle Paul prays that we may be sanctified and preserved blameless; then it is a matter of absolute indifference what anyone thinks of us, but it is not a matter of indifference what God's Holy Spirit thinks of us.

If we are sanctified by the power of the God of peace, our self-life is blameless before Him. There is nothing to hide; and the more we bring our soul under the searchlight of God, the more we realize the ineffable comfort of the supernatural work He has done.

Of ourselves we can never be any of the things God says we must be. We can never be blameless by thinking about it, or by praying about it, but only by being sanctified, and that is God's absolute sovereign work of grace. "Abraham believed God, and it was accounted to him for righteousness" (Galatians 3:6). Do I believe God can sanctify me? "Christ Jesus . . . became for us . . . sanctification" (1 Corinthians 1:30). Have we the quiet confidence of a child that the life of Jesus Christ can be formed in us until the relationship to God of spirit, soul, and body is without blame before Him? It is not the perfection of attainment in thinking, or in bodily life, or in worship, but the perfection of a blameless disposition, nothing in it to censure, and that in the eyes of God who sees everything.

Is it possible to be blameless in our self-life? Paul says it is, and the writer to the Hebrews states that it is by sanctification we are made one with Jesus. "For both He who sanctifies and those who are being sanctified are all of one" (Hebrews 2:11). That is the glorious work of Jesus Christ in our life. Has He performed His work in us or has He not? Do not ask anybody else about it; the Holy Spirit will show you as clearly as can be. If you are right with God, you would not thank the angel Gabriel for telling you, because you know it. It will be the witness not of a word only, but nothing less than absolute agreement with God's standard when He brings you up against it.

## To Be Blameless in My Social Life?

That you may become blameless and harmless, children of God without fault, in the midst of a crooked and perverse generation, among whom you shine as lights in the world. (Philippians 2:15)

Am I without blame in relation to my father and mother, to my wife or husband, my brothers and sisters? If the work of Jesus Christ has had its way in us, God Almighty can see nothing to censure when He scrutinizes us by His Holy Spirit. The Spirit of God does not work as our minds do; that is, He does not work with suspicion. He works silently and gently as daylight. There will be a check here, an illumination there, a wonderful all-over realization—"Thank God, He has done it!" There is no need to protest or to profess. We have to be blameless in all our social relationships before God, but that will not mean that our relations will think us blameless! We can always gauge where we are by the teachings of Jesus Christ.

Is it possible to be blameless in our social life? The apostle Paul says it is, and if we were asked whether we believed God could make us blameless, we would all say, "Yes." Well, has He done it? If God has not sanctified us and made us blameless, there is only one reason He has not—we do not want Him to. "For this is the will of God, your sanctification" (1 Thessalonians 4:3). We do not have to urge God to do it; it is His will. Is it our will? Sanctification is the work of the supernatural power of God.

## To Be Blameless in My Spiritual Life?

He chose us in Him before the foundation of the world, that we should be holy and without blame before Him in love. (Ephesians 1:4)

Therefore, beloved, looking forward to these things, be diligent to be found by Him in peace, without spot and blameless. (2 Peter 3:14)

Is it possible to be blameless in our spiritual relationship to almighty God, to Jesus Christ, and to the Holy Spirit? It is not only possible, but God's word tells us that is what God does: "If we walk in the light as He is in the light . . . the blood of Jesus Christ His Son cleanses us from all sin" (1 John 1:7). That is cleansing not from conscious sin only but from infinitely more; it is cleansing to the depths of crystalline purity so that God Himself can see nothing impure. That is the work of the Lord Jesus Christ; to make His work anything less would be blasphemous. If God Almighty cannot do that in your life and mine, we have followed "cunningly devised fables" (2 Peter 1:16). Unless Jesus Christ can remake Himself in us, what is the meaning of those thirty years in Nazareth, those three years of His public life? What is the meaning of the cross of Jesus Christ, of His resurrection and ascension, if He cannot cleanse us from all sin? But, bless God, He can! The point is—have we let Him do it?

Beware of praising Jesus Christ whilst all the time you cunningly refuse to let the Spirit of God work His salvation efficaciously in your life. Remember, the battle is in the will; whenever we say "I can't," or whenever we are indifferent, it means "I won't." It is better to let Jesus Christ uncover the obstinacy. If there is one point where we say "I won't," then we shall never know His salvation. From the moment that God uncovers a point of obstinacy in us and we refuse to let Him deal with it, we begin to be skeptical, to sneer and watch for defects in the lives of others. But when once we yield to Him entirely, He makes us blameless in our personal life, in our practical life, and in our profound life. It is not done by piety; it is wrought in us by the sovereign grace of God, and we have not the slightest desire to trust in ourselves in any degree, but in Him alone.

"Now to Him who is able to keep you from stumbling, and to present you faultless before the presence of His glory with exceeding joy" (Jude 24). Can God keep me from stumbling this second? Yes. Can He keep me from sin this second? Yes. Well, that is the whole of life; you cannot live more than a second at a time. If God can keep you blameless this second, He can do it the next. No wonder Jesus Christ said, "Let not your heart be troubled" (John 14:27)! We do get troubled when we do not remember the amazing power of God.

# WILL YOU GO OUT
# WITHOUT KNOWING?

Abraham . . . went out, not knowing where he was going.
Hebrews 11:8

That is true either of a fool or a faithful soul. One of the hardest
lessons to learn is this one that Abraham's life brings out. He went
out of all his own ways of looking at things and became a fool in the
eyes of the world.

## Out in Separation unto God

Now the LORD had said to Abram: "Get out of your country, from your family and from your father's house, to a
land that I will show you. (Genesis 12:1)

Have you been "out" in that way? If you have, there is no logi-
cal statement possible if anyone asks what you are doing. Suppose
you are asked why you are in this college, that job, or that circumstance? You do not know, and you ought not to know. One of the
greatest difficulties in Christian work is that everyone says, "Now

what do you expect to do?" Of course you do not know what you are going to do. The only thing you know is that God knows what He is about.

Separation unto God is the first characteristic—separation unto God for food, for clothing, for money, for the next step. It is a "going out" of all your "family" and "house" ways of looking at things—a "going out" with nothing in view, but being perfectly certain that you are separated unto God. "Beloved, do not think it strange," says Peter, "concerning the fiery trial which is to try you, as though some strange thing happened to you: but rejoice . . . " (1 Peter 4:12–13). Whenever you have been faithful to God, you do not know you have been faithful until it is pointed out, and you say, "Why, I never thought of that as a test." It is only on looking back that you find it was.

We have continually to revise our attitude toward God and see if it is a "going out"—out of everything, trusting in God entirely. It is this attitude that keeps us in perpetual wonder. We know God, and we know He is a supernatural God who works miracles, and our attitude is one of childlike amazement: "I don't know what God is going to do next." A child sees giants and fairies where we see only the most prosaic things. Jesus said, "unless you . . . become as little children" (Matthew 18:3). Every morning we wake it is to be a "going out," building in confidence on God. "Therefore I say to you, do not worry about your life, what you will eat or what you will drink; nor about your body, what you will put on" (Matthew 6:25). Take no thought, that is, for anything you did take thought for before you "went out." Before you "went out" you did take thought for your life, for what you should do tomorrow, but now you belong to the crowd Jesus Christ heads, and you seek first the kingdom of God and His righteousness.

## Out in Surrender to God

I will make you a great nation; I will bless you and make your name great; and you shall be a blessing. (Genesis 12:2)

It means more to surrender to God for Him to do a big thing than to surrender a big thing to God. We have to surrender our common, ordinary little notions for a tremendous revelation that takes our breath away. For instance, am I humble enough to accept the tremendous revelation that God Almighty, the Lord Jesus Christ, and the Holy Spirit will come and make Their abode with me (see John 14:23)? Will I so completely surrender the sense of my own unworthiness that I go out of all my own ways of thinking and let God do exactly as He likes?

Sacrifice in the Bible means that we give to God the best we have; it is the finest form of worship. Sacrifice is not giving up things, but giving to God with joy the best we have. We have dragged down the idea of surrender and of sacrifice. We have taken the life out of the words and made them mean something sad and weary and despicable. In the Bible they mean the very opposite. To go out in surrender to God means the surrendering of the miserable sense of my own unimportance. Am I willing to surrender that ordinary, ignoble little sense for the great big idea God has for me? Am I willing to surrender the fact that I am an ignorant, useless, worthless, too-old person? There is more hindrance to God's work because people cling to a sense of unworthiness than because of conceit.

"Who am I?" Instantly the trend of the mind is to say, "Oh, well, I have not had any education," or, "I did not begin soon enough." Am I willing to surrender the whole thing and go out in surrender to God? To go out of the carnal mind into the spiritual? "Being fools for Christ's sake"?

Abraham surrendered himself entirely to the supernatural God. Have you got hold of a supernatural God? Not, do you know what God is going to do? You cannot know, but you have faith in Him, and therefore He can do what He likes. Has God been trying to bring into your life the fact that He is supernatural, and have you been asking Him what He is going to do? He will never tell you. God does not tell us what He is going to do; He reveals to us who He is (see John 14:12–13).

Do you believe in a miracle-working God, and will you go out in surrender to Him? Have you faith in your holiness or in God? Faith in your obedience or in God? Have you gone out in surrender to God until you would not be surprised at anything He did? No one is surprised over what God does when once he has faith in Him. Have you a supernatural God, or do you tie Him up by the laws of your own mind?

We blunder mostly on the line of surrender, not of conceit, in the continual reminders we give to God that we are small and mean. We are much worse than small and mean. Jesus said, "Without Me you can do nothing" (John 15:5). Let us surrender all thinking about ourselves either for appreciation or depreciation, cast ourselves confidently on God, and go out like children.

## Out in Sanctification for God

So Abram departed [went out] as the LORD had spoken to him. (Genesis 12:4)

Sanctification means going out as God has told us. Are we going along the line God has told us in the things we have been saying and thinking, in letter writing, in prayer with people in difficulty? If it is a matter of our own personal sanctification, let us put God between ourselves and the difficulty.

Our Lord did not rebuke His disciples for making mistakes, but for not having faith. The two things that astonished Him were "little faith" and "great faith." Faith is not in what Jesus Christ can do, but in Himself, and anything He can do is less than Himself.

Suppose that God is the God we know Him to be when we are nearest to Him. What an impertinence worry is! Think of the unspeakable marvel of the remaining hours of this day, and think how easily we can shut God right out of His universe by the logic of our own heads, by a trick of our nerves, by remembering the way we have limited Him in the past—banish Him right out, and let the old worry and care come in, until we are a disgrace to the name of Jesus. But let the attitude be a continual "going out" in dependence on God and the life will have an ineffable charm, which is a satisfaction to Jesus Christ.

We have to learn how to "go out" of everything—out of convictions, out of creeds, out of experiences, out of everything—until so far as our faith is concerned, there is nothing between us and God.

# Do You Continue to Go with Jesus?

Ye are they which have continued with Me in My temptations. (Luke 22:28 KJV)

We are apt to imagine that our Lord was only tempted once, and then His temptations were over. His temptations went on from the first moment of His conscious life to the last, because His holiness was not the holiness of almighty God, but the holiness of man, which can only progress by means of the things that go against it (see Hebrews 2:18; 4:15). Are we going with Jesus in His temptations? It is true that He is with us in our temptations, but are we with Him in His? Many of us cease to go with Jesus from the moment we have an experience of what He can do. Like Peter, we have all had moments when Jesus has had to say to us, "What? Could you not watch with Me one hour?" (Matthew 26:40).

Are we lazy spiritually because we are so active in God's work? When the problems of the body face us, do we stop going with Jesus? Do we listen to the tempter's voice to put our bodily needs first: "Eat bread, be well, first look after what you are going to wear, and then attend to God"? It is the most subtle voice any Christian ever heard, and whether it comes through an archangel or through a man or woman, it is the voice of the devil. Are we going with Jesus along these lines, or are we putting our own needs and the needs of men and social reform first?

Satan does not come on the line of tempting us to sin, but on the line of making us shift our point of view, and only the Spirit of God can detect this as a temptation of the devil. It is the same in missionary enterprise and in all Christian work. The church is apt not to go with Jesus in His temptations. The temptations of our Lord in the days of His flesh are the kinds of temptations He is subjected to in the temple of our body. Watch when God shifts your circumstances and see whether you are going with Jesus or siding with the world, the flesh, and the devil. We wear His badge, but are we going with Him? "From that time many of His disciples went back and walked with Him no more" (John 6:66).

The temptation may be to do some big startling thing in order to prove that we really are the children of God. Satan said to Jesus, "If You are the Son of God, throw Yourself down" (Matthew 4:6). To us he says, "If you are saved and sanctified and true to God, everyone you know should be saved too." If that were true, Jesus Christ is wrong in His revelation of God. If by our salvation and right relationship to God we can be the means of turning our world upside down, what has Jesus Christ been doing all these years? The temptation is to claim that God does something that will prove who we are and what He has done for us. It is a temptation of the devil, and can only be detected as a temptation by the Spirit of God.

Are we taking the pattern and print of our life from some booklet or some band of Christians, or are we continuing with Jesus, standing with Him in every new circumstance of life? It is there that we understand the fellowship of His sufferings, and the broader He makes our life and our mind and circumstances, the more essential does the one thing become—to continue with Him in His temptations.

Have we given God as much "elbow room" in our lives as our Lord gave Him in His? Have we the one set purpose, which is only born in us by the Son of God, namely, not to do our own will but the will of God—"that the life of Jesus also may be manifested in our mortal flesh" (2 Corinthians 4:11)? The temptations of Jesus continued all His earthly life, and they will continue all the time of His life in us. Are we going with Jesus in the life we are living now?

The temptation may be to compromise with evil: "Don't be so tremendously strong against sin and in denouncing the pleasures and interests that make up this life as it is, and the whole world will be at your feet." Jesus Christ was tempted like His brethren (see Hebrews 4:15), not like men who are not born again. When we are tempted as He was, do we continue to go with Him? What are we like where nobody sees? Have we a place in our heart and mind and life where there is always open communion between ourselves and God so that we can detect the voice of the devil when he comes as "an angel of light"?

Every temptation of the devil is full of the most amazing wisdom and the understanding of every problem that ever stretched before men's view. Satan's kingdom is based on wisdom; along the lines he advocates lies success, and men recognize this. Jesus Christ is not on the line of success but on the spiritual line—the holy, practical line and no other. If men and women do not continue to go with Jesus, they will begin to teach what undermines the kingdom of Jesus Christ.

"Ye are they which have continued with Me in My temptations" (Luke 22:28 KJV). Are we compromising in the tiniest degree in mental concept with forces that do not continue to go with Jesus, or are we maintaining the attitude of Jesus Christ all through? Are we departing from Jesus in the slightest way in connection with the world to which we belong? Have we this past week choked the Son of God in our life by imperceptible degrees? Have the demands of the life of the Son of God in us been a bit too spiritual, too strong, too sternly holy, too sternly unworldly, too pressing, too narrow, too much in the eye of God only? Or do we say, "Yes, Lord, I'll go with You all the way"?

> I have made my choice for ever,
> I will walk with Christ my Lord.

Watch where Jesus went. The one dominant note in His life was to do His Father's will. His is not the way of wisdom or of success, but the way of faithfulness.

No matter what your circumstances may be, don't try to shield yourself from things God is bringing into your life. We have the idea sometimes that we ought to shield ourselves from some of the circumstances God brings round us. Never! God engineers circumstances; we have to see that we face them abiding continually with Him in His temptations. They are *His* temptations, they are not temptations to us, but to the Son of God in us. If you talk about the subtle temptations that come to you as a child of God to those who have not the life of the Son of God, they will laugh at you. We continually side with the prince of this world and have to be brought back to a spiritual stocktaking. Are we going with Jesus in His temptations in our bodies? Are we going with Him in the temptations of our mental and moral life, and of our spiritual life, abiding true to God all through? That is the one concern Jesus Christ has about us.

"Ye are they which have continued with Me in My temptations." Do you continue to go with Jesus? The way lies through Gethsemane, through the city gate, outside the camp. The way lies alone, and the way lies until there is no trace of a footstep left, only the voice—"Follow Me."

"As He is, so are we in this world" (1 John 4:17). Where is Jesus in this world? There is no outward manifestation of Jesus, and we are to be as He is, hidden, true, and absolutely loyal to God. Temptations do not come in fits and starts; they abide all the time. And to continue with Jesus in them is the way the holiness of our life is going to be to the glory of God.

# NOTE TO THE READER

The publisher invites you to share your response to the message of this book by writing Discovery House Publishers, P.O. Box 3566, Grand Rapids, MI 49501, U.S.A. For information about other Discovery House books, music, videos, or DVDs, contact us at the same address or call 1-800-653-8333. Find us on the Internet at http://www.dhp.org/ or send e-mail to books@dhp.org.